# CHINA'S POLITICAL REFORMS

# CHINA'S POLITICAL REFORMS

## An Interim Report

BENEDICT STAVIS

 PRAEGER

New York
Westport, Connecticut
London

Passages from the Spring 1987 (Volume XX, No. 1) issue of *Chinese Law and Government* reprinted by permission of M.E. Sharpe, Inc., Armonk, New York 10504.

**Library of Congress Cataloging-in-Publication Data**

Stavis, Benedict.
    China's political reforms.

    Bibliography: p.
    Includes index.
    1. China—Politics and government—1976–
I. Title.
DS779.26.S75      1988        320.951        87–7184
ISBN 0–275–92905–1 (alk. paper)

Library of Congress Catalog Card Number: 87–7184

ISBN: 0–275–92905–1

First published in 1988

Praeger Publishers, One Madison Avenue, New York, NY 10010
A division of Greenwood Press, Inc.

Printed in the United States of America

The paper used in this book complies with the
Permanent Paper Standard issued by the National
Information Standards Organization (Z39.48-1984).

10  9  8  7  6  5  4  3  2  1

# Contents

# *Preface and*
# *Acknowledgments*

When I accepted an invitation to teach political science in Shanghai, China in fall 1986, I knew it was going to be an exciting time. I had been studying, researching, and teaching about China for decades. I had toured in China twice before, and had worked on two occasions with the Chinese government on agricultural development projects. But this was the first time I would be teaching in China. Best of all, I would be teaching political science, a new academic discipline in China, at Fudan University, a premier university, precisely at the time of discussion on political reform.

My experience was even better than I had hoped. It turned out that 1986/87 was a vintage year for Chinese politics. When I arrived in September, the Chinese official press was filled with penetrating denunciations of China's dictatorial political system, and optimistic calls for democratic reform. Then tremendous student demonstrations took place in Shanghai and dozens of other Chinese cities. My students went from my lectures on comparative politics to the streets, demanding democracy and human rights. For this I take no credit or blame. My students were no more radical than hundreds of thousands of others. Indeed, my students were probably more cautious and more aware of the problems of rapid political reform. My colleagues shook their heads in amazement. Then, suddenly, the conservative forces struck back. The head of the Chinese Communist Party was forced to resign, and everyone wondered how far the political pendulum would swing.

I left China then, at the end of the semester, as scheduled. I knew I had been in China at a historical moment. This book represents my desire to understand more completely what was happening while I was there, and to share with others the good fortune of being in the right place at the right time.

Much of this book was written in Shanghai from September 1986 to January 1987. However, upon coming home, I found in the library many documents, insights, and analyses that were not available to me in China. These materials were very helpful in understanding elite factional politics. My friends and colleagues in China appear in retrospect to have been largely ignorant about this topic, or at least reluctant to share with me what they knew. The reports available outside China were written by international journalists in China who obtained detailed descriptions and internal documents from high-level sources. Most of their stories turned out to be accurate predictions of events. Indeed, in May 1987 a Japanese reporter was expelled from China for obtaining secret documents, thereby confirming the accuracy of the source material of the international journalists.[1] In addition, some of Deng's important speeches, which were secret and unavailable when I was in China, were published after I returned home.

This book combines these documentary sources with the insights and perspectives that came from extensive personal contact in China. I have not attempted to cite every discussion with every colleague and student. To do so would intrude on the privacy of professional relationships. I am happy to acknowledge that these discussions have contributed a great deal to my understanding of China.

For this reason, my deepest thanks go to my colleagues and students in the Department of International Politics at Fudan University. My department gave me full freedom to teach Comparative Politics and Research Methods as I would in the United States. Many colleagues were extremely generous with their time, helping me to understand different aspects of China. Students helped me translate many of the important articles on political reform, which are being published elsewhere.[2] Students and colleagues were all wonderful in asking those penetrating questions that force one to rethink and reorder thoughts.

Special thanks go to the university president, Prof. Xie Xide, her administration, and Fudan's Office of Foreign Affairs for providing an environment of serious intellectual inquiry. They all labored to solve numerous small problems, so that I (and all of us "foreign experts") could concentrate on our work. Library staff were very helpful also.

Some ideas in this book emerged from numerous delightful conversations with Prof. Jerry Ravitz, visiting at Fudan's Philosophy Department from Leeds University.

When I returned to Iowa, I was fortunate to be a scholar at the Center of Asian and Pacific Studies of the University of Iowa. I am deeply indebted to the Center for providing me a supportive environment in which to complete the manuscript. I am especially thankful to Prof. David

Arkush and Margaret Thompson for close readings of the manuscript and numerous suggestions. I also received encouragement and helpful suggestions from Prof. Michel Oksenberg of the University of Michigan, for which I am most thankful.

All my colleagues and friends may take credit for any thoughtful comments this book offers. Of course, I take full responsibility for all errors in fact and interpretation.

Finally, emotional support from my family, including wife, son, and parents has been crucial at every stage of the writing of this book, both while I was in China and at home.

## NOTES

1. "Japanese journalist ordered to leave," *Beijing Review*, no. 20 (May 18, 1987), pp. 8–9.

2. Benedict Stavis, "Reform of China's political system," *Chinese Law and Government*, 20:1 (Spring 1987).

# CHINA'S
# POLITICAL REFORMS

# Introduction

Can a proletarian dictatorship, such as China, based on an ideology of Marxism-Leninism, transform itself and become democratic? Many observers think that communist systems cannot change their basic natures.[1] They are inherently stable and unchangeable, because the rulers and communist parties have total control over ideology, the political system, and the economy, and are willing to use coercion.[2] Authoritarian political culture is deeply imbued in both leaders and masses. The power of the state comes from its own ideology and organization, and from its ability to penetrate and control society.

The Soviet Union is a prime example. Reform has been desperately necessary. Numerous scholars have detailed the complex problems emerging in the Soviet Union and, by extension, in other communist systems. Rigid bureaucratic control of the economy has created economic stagnation. The highly regulated social environment has generated despair, alienation, alcoholism, and deterioration of family stability. Intellectual life has been clouded by the ever-present KGB with its informers, gulag, and psychiatric hospitals. Top nuclear scientists have been in prison camps knitting sweaters, not in laboratories helping to prevent the next nuclear pollution disaster. Political alienation has been obvious and widespread.[3] Ethnic tensions have increased as the non-Russian portion of the population has expanded.[4]

Nevertheless, despite these problems, observers still emphasized the obstacles to change. The Soviet leadership was judged incapable of allowing change that might involve foreign military disadvantage. Nor would it tolerate any weakening of domestic communist party control. Only cosmetic reform seemed possible.[5]

This analysis has strong historical logic. No socialist system based on Marxism has established a model for broad, institutionalized, political participation that would enable society to control the state. The concrete historical circumstances under which communist political systems have been established have not been conducive to democracy. One pattern, apparent in the Soviet Union, China, and Vietnam, has been that Marxist revolutions have occurred in poor countries with strong bureaucratic traditions and authoritarian political cultures. Revolutions were successful at times when the countries were engaged in, and weakened by, major international conflicts. These revolutions seized power through military struggle, so military values and organizational patterns shaped their political systems. Alternatively, Marxist governments have been imposed by external military force, as in East Europe. Neither of these patterns is conducive to the development of democracy. No communist system has successfully made a transition to a political system that has extensive participation in decision making, and that has stable institutions and laws.[6]

On the other hand, there is important evidence that communist political systems are not really so stable. The great power of the communist state is actually a double-edged sword. The state can shape society, but it cannot avoid responsibility for all the problems that emerge. It cannot blame market conditions, legal constraints, or anything else (except for the imperialists and capitalists). Governmental strength paradoxically becomes a weakness.[7] Domestic political forces actually overthrew the communist systems in Hungary in 1956, in Czechoslovakia in 1968, and in Poland in 1981. Only direct foreign military intervention or martial law kept the communist governments in power.

The Eastern European communist countries have attempted some reform. Hungary has introduced markets to some degree and has experimented with some reform in the electoral process. Yugoslavia has for many years given much control of the workplace to the workers themselves. However, in the past, the reforms in Eastern Europe have been basically restricted to those that the Soviet Union would allow. The communist world has had substantial interest and discussion about reform, even though little reform has been implemented.

China's communist political system has been as resistant to change as the other communist systems. China's political system was established by the Chinese Communist Party in 1949. It is based on communist party leadership of all political activities. This is the most important of the "four cardinal principles" of the system. Under party control, executive, legislative, and judicial institutions are virtually merged, and cannot function independently or offer any form of checks and balances over the top leaders.

The party also organizes and controls groups and potential groups, such as farmers, factory workers, and professionals. This prevents the groups from developing independent bases of political power. The system bears some resemblance to the corporatist system of political organization.

China's political system has popular participation, but the participation is weak, not independent, and not institutionalized. At the highest levels, the top few dozen political leaders have substantial freedom to put forward conflicting ideas. They are responsive to a wide range of pressures. They each take frequent inspection tours, and meet with local officials, technicians, and others. They send down inspection teams and maintain networks of personal contacts through friends, relatives, and close associates. They respond to letters to newspapers, social surveys and to public demonstrations (which are infrequent but not unknown). While there is extensive participation, it is organized and controlled by party leaders, and cannot become part of an independent political movement. The leaders ultimately make decisions behind closed doors, in ways that remain obscure to the Chinese themselves.

China's legal framework is weak. It has been a government by official fiat and a government by people, not by law. Law has been one element of state controlling society, not a way society controls the state. High level government officials have directed judges' decisions. Freedom has been constrained, and a wide range of punishments, ranging from bad work assignments and lack of promotion to prison and worse, have awaited those who stepped outside the boundaries of permissible public comment or political activity.

After Mao Zedong's death, some Chinese intellectuals and workers talked about change. The political system had brought severe economic and social dislocation and widespread violence and brutality. To prevent repetition of this, they openly discussed democracy. Beginning in November 1978, highly critical posters were glued up and not torn down by government workers. The wall on which they were posted became known as "Democracy Wall," and the groups of people who came to discuss the ideas became known as the Democracy Movement. Over the next two years, more than 150 unofficial journals emerged to explore new political ideas.[8] After five months, the government began to tighten up. On March 30, 1979, Deng Xiaoping laid down the limits to dissent in four cardinal points: 1) keep to the socialist road; 2) uphold the dictatorship of the proletariat; 3) uphold the leadership of the communist party; and 4) uphold Marxism-Leninism and Mao Zedong thought.[9] In April, leaders of the democracy movement were arrested. In October 1979 an important leader, Wei Jingsheng, was sentenced to fifteen years in prison, and the next month the Democracy Wall was closed. In addition, unofficial publications were closed down.

Some participants in the battered Democracy Movement turned to electoral politics. In Spring 1980, local elections were held for representatives to local People's Congresses. Some progressive candidates won, particularly on university campuses. Other activists started to form Polish-style free trade unions.

That was too much for the communist leadership. In early 1981 the government clamped down, and by spring, many activists and writers were jailed. Trials in the summer of 1982 brought 10–15 year sentences. The Democracy Movement seemed crushed.[10] The permanent nature of Chinese communism seemed confirmed. Because this movement was based in Beijing and was reported in great detail by Western journalists, it is well known in the West, but details of it are not very well known in other regions of China.

Nevertheless, political reform arose phoenix-like in 1986. Important top leaders and younger intellectuals allied to advocate structural reform and democratization of the political system. China's top political scientists began to present a more pluralistic image of society with conflicting interests. They implied that the autonomous state was not strong but weak because it brought economic inefficiency and lacked political legitimacy. Progressive articles were published in official periodicals, not in privately mimeographed shoestring magazines. Then widespread student demonstrations for democracy and human rights shook the country in December 1986.

The demonstrations showed that the young generations, brought up in the communist era, had a different political outlook from older generations. This new political generation saw the communist party as a ruling establishment, responsible for all problems. They did not view the communist party as the revolutionary group that had saved or would save the country from the problems of poverty, feudalism, and imperialist invasion, as their parents might have. Youth wanted a new political compact.

Some of the senior officials understood this and vigorously supported reform. Other leaders had different ideas for reform. All wanted to reform fast enough to maintain the confidence of youth, and to ensure that the party would lead the change, not try to block it. They wanted a more efficient, more popular communist system. They did not want the party to be capsized by the waves of change. Inspired by reforms in Eastern European socialist countries but having no satisfactory, concrete model from the communist world, China's reformers sometimes considered the Meiji Restoration in Japan in the late 19th century as an example of successful top-down reform.[11] Some reformers, however, wanted to go farther. They wanted a fundamental change in the communist authoritarian system. Tensions grew between these two perspectives of reform.

Conservative forces, generally representing the older leaders who had made the revolution four decades earlier, put clear limits on reform in January 1987. Hu Yaobang, the general secretary of the Communist Party, was forced to resign, and China entered an extended period of criticism against "bourgeois liberalization." The pluralist vision of politics was rejected, leaving by default the politics of state control by the party elite.

Critics would say that the goal of the conservative reformers was to establish "rational totalitarianism." Such a political system is characterized by less brutal elite struggle, more relaxed control at the grassroots level, support of intellectuals, encouragement of political apathy, and greater freedom in personal lifestyle, art, and religion. Nevertheless, the system maintains control over the media, represses independent political parties and movements, and selects its own leaders through a patronage system.[12]

What are the prospects for Chinese reform? With Deng Xiaoping 82 years old, succession issues will be intertwined with complex factional struggles.[13] Those conflicts may preempt substantive political reform for a few years. Moreover, conservative leaders deny the existence of conflicting interests or factions.[14] This perspective reduces the legitimacy of popular participation in politics, and leaves politics as an elite, autonomous activity.

These words are written just prior to the Thirteenth National Party Congress of the Chinese Communist Party, planned for October, 1987. Political reform is expected to be the major issue at that meeting. The congress will probably agree on those limited reforms Deng endorses and on which there is a widespread consensus in China. These reforms will include personnel decisions to bring younger people with fresh ideas into leadership positions; efforts to streamline party and government organs, including sharper separation of their responsibilities; and more delegation of power to lower levels to generate more initiative. Even these minor changes are considered controversial in China, and will take five to ten years to implement. Major, structural changes, such as the introduction of a multi-party system and the separation of executive, legislative, and judicial powers, clearly will not be made now.[15] Whether they will be made in the future will be decided by future generations.

Whatever happens in the short-term, the underlying structural reasons for reform, which were so obvious in 1979 and again in 1986, can only become stronger as years go by. Discussions, experiments, and demonstrations for political reform may resume in a few years. Over a period of a few years, some political reforms will be implemented to make the existing system more stable and efficient. The more complicated question is the outlook over several decades. Will a rationalized communist system be a stable political form, or will its own internal contradictions set the stage for further democratic evolution over the following decades? There is little historical experience to use in reaching an answer to this question.

The need to think in terms of decades is frustrating, but in fact is consistent with the historical experiences of other countries, as they have transformed themselves from authoritarian to democratic systems. Most democratic transformations have required decades or centuries. This is the time frame many people in China use. They liken China to a huge, overcrowded train with a billion passengers, approaching a switch in the tracks. Straight ahead leads to a washed-out bridge. The other track is the only safe course. When such a train changes its course, it must do so very carefully and gradually. Otherwise, it will derail, creating a great disaster. We need only think of the political evolution of Germany, Italy, Argentina, and Japan during this century, to see the truth of this insight.

The Chinese discussions of reform are taking place in the context of a broader reform movement in the world socialist movement. Chinese reform received inspirations from reform activities in Eastern Europe, in particular from Hungary, and to some extent from Yugoslavia and Romania. In turn, the Soviet Union and Vietnam have announced major reform programs in early 1987, which bear some similarity to Chinese reforms. Mikhail Gorbachev's highly public announcement of reforms in February 1987 and the symbolic release of many political prisoners suggests that the Soviet Union may now be making a serious attempt at reform. Soviet reforms will in turn enable more reform in Eastern Europe.

In China, reforms have met obstacles and resistance. The same is inevitable in the Soviet Union. In both countries, the forces for and against reform are engaged in protracted battle. Immediate, thorough, institutionalized reform is not likely in either country. The key question is whether reforms can be implemented over a lengthy time period.

It is possible that we are witnessing the beginnings of major structural changes in the Leninist model of socialism that has characterized Marxist orthodoxy for the past six decades. Marxist opposition parties in Western Europe have transformed into pragmatic, democratic parties. Can a ruling communist system do the same?

## NOTES

1. The word "communist" is used here in the Western sense of a government with a Marxist ideology and under the leadership of a Leninist party. Communist governments always point out that from a Marxist perspective, their social systems are not "communist." Communism may come in the distant future, when the economy is developed and people's consciousness changes. At present, they

consider themselves to be socialist, not communist. China now says it is only at the initial stage of socialism.

2. Carl Friederich and Zbigniew Brzezinski, *Totalitarian Dictatorship and Autocracy* (Cambridge, MA: Harvard University Press, 1956).

3. James Cracraft, "A Soviet turning point," *Bulletin of the Atomic Scientists* (Feb. 1986), pp. 8–12.

4. Timothy Colton, *Dilemma of Reform in the Soviet Union* (New York: Council on Foreign Relations, 1984).

5. Robert Byrnes, "Change in the Soviet political system: Limits and likelihoods," *Review of Politics* (Oct. 1984), pp. 502–15.

6. Jeane Kirkpatrick, *Dictatorships and Double Standards* (New York: Simon and Schuster, 1982).

7. Hugh Berrington, "British government, the paradox of strength," in Dennis Kavanagh and Gillian Peele (eds.), *Comparative Government and Politics* (Boulder, CO: Westview Press, 1984), pp. 20–47.

8. James Tong (ed.), "Underground journals in China," *Chinese Law and Government*, 13:3–4 (Fall/Winter 1980/81).

9. "Uphold the four cardinal principles," *Selected Works of Deng Xiaoping (1975–1982)* (Beijing: Foreign Languages Press, 1984), p. 172.

10. Andrew Nathan, *Chinese Democracy* (New York: Knopf, 1985); Roger Garside, *Coming Alive, China After Mao* (New York: McGraw Hill, 1981); David Goodman, *Beijing Street Voices: The Poetry and Politics of China's Democracy Movement* (Boston: M. Boyars, 1981); James Seymour, *The Fifth Modernization: China's Human Rights Movement* (Standfordville, NY: Human Rights Publishing Group, 1980); Robin Munro, "Chen Erjin and the Chinese Democracy Movement," in Chen Erjin, *China: Crossroads Socialism* (London: Verso, 1984), pp. 6–15.

11. "The past week," *Ta Kung Pao* (Jan. 8–14, 1987), p. 2; FBIS (Jan. 8, 1987), p. K 18.

12. Dong Xusheng, "China: toward rational totalitarianism?" *China Spring Digest* (Jan./Feb. 1987), pp. 54–62.

13. Dong Xusheng, "Who's who in Deng and Chen factions," *China Spring Digest* (Jan./Feb. 1987), pp. 18–24.

14. "The 'conservative'/'reformist' myth," *Beijing Review*, no. 17 (April 27, 1987), pp. 4–5.

15. "Deng calls for speedup in reform," *Beijing Review*, no. 34 (August 24, 1987), pp. 15–16.

# 1
## Reasons for Reform

In 1986 China was buzzing with talk about reform of the political system (*zhengzhi tizhi gaige*). Top leaders and academics detailed the shortcomings in the existing system and outlined ideas for reforms to make the system more democratic. Three reasons converged to make political reforms seem necessary. Economic reforms required complementary political reforms; China's political system needed an overhaul to reverse the deterioration of its legitimacy; and new political values were emerging in China's younger generation.

## CALL FOR REFORM

Deng Xiaoping, China's top leader, gave legitimacy to discussion of political reform in his speech of August 1980, "On the Reform of the System of Party and State Leadership." Deng's goals may have been simply to provide a theoretical justification for purging his opponents, but the speech went beyond personal criticism, and bluntly exposed China's political system:

As far as the leadership and cadre systems of our Party and state are concerned, the major problems are bureaucracy, over-concentration of power, patriarchal methods, life tenure in leading posts and privileges of various kinds.

Bureaucracy remains a major and widespread problem in the political life of our Party and state. Its harmful manifestations include the following: standing high above the masses; abusing power; divorcing oneself from reality and the masses; spending a lot of time and effort to put up an impressive front; indulging in empty talk; sticking to a rigid way of thinking; being hidebound by convention; overstaffing administrative organs; being dilatory, inefficient, and irresponsible;

failing to keep one's word; circulating documents endlessly without solving problems; shifting responsibility to others; and even assuming the airs of a mandarin, reprimanding other people at every turn, vindictively attacking others, suppressing democracy, deceiving superiors and subordinates, being arbitrary and despotic, practising favoritism, offering bribes, participating in corrupt practices in violation of the law, and so on. Such things have reached *intolerable dimensions* both in our domestic affairs and in our contacts with other countries. (emphasis added)

Continuing, Deng thought that these problems had roots both in China's history of a centralized emperor and in the traditional socialist model of development:

Bureaucracy is an age-old and complex historical phenomenon. In addition to sharing some common characteristics with past types of bureaucracy, Chinese bureaucracy in its present form has characteristics of its own. That is, it differs from both the bureaucracy of old China and that prevailing in the capitalist countries. It is closely connected with our highly centralized management in the economic, political, cultural and social fields, which we have long regarded as essential for the socialist system and for planning... [1]

It must be recognized that a speech like this is not a simple personal statement by one person, any more than the U.S. president's Economic Report is a personal statement. Deng's speech on political reform reflected extensive surveys and discussion by research and policy units within the highest levels of the Central Committee. It symbolized a fundamental institutional decision that political reforms were needed.

Of course this analysis had its own background. After Mao's death in 1976, there was widespread public revelation of the horrible violence of the cultural revolution (1966–1976) and of economic stagnation.[2] China's political system had not been able to prevent these tragedies. The Democracy Wall movement was an independent, popular attempt of Chinese to find a new political solution. Deng's statement was part of this effort to understand China's political system and to make sure that past errors were not repeated. Its timing makes it appear that Deng wanted to cover up or counterbalance the fact that China had already restricted, arrested, and jailed the leaders of that movement, and to take political initiative from them.

Deng's shocking admissions were at a closed-door meeting and were not published until 1983. For a few years, the narrower, simpler implications of the report about the cadre system were discussed, and various steps were taken in this regard. Large scale conferences were held, under the auspices of local social science academies to review problems in public administration.

The broader implications of the report were emphasized again in

1986. In April, Deng spoke to a conference of provincial governors, and reiterated these views.[3] Vice Premier Wan Li also gave a speech in April 1986, indicating that reform of the political system was an issue to be discussed. This speech was an internal party document, and was not published at the time. Deng gave further impetus to the movement for political reform in a speech on June 20, to a conference on party work style. This speech was a "bugle call" for political structural reform.[4] Deng told the Standing Committee of the Political Bureau on June 28:

... it is necessary to pay attention to reform of the political structure... I think all comrades, particularly comrades of the Secretariat, should consider the problem of the reform of the political structure.

Reforming the economic structure without revamping the political structure will simply not work...

The party should handle things relating to party discipline, and whatever comes under the law should be handled by the state and government.[5]

During this time period, discussions were conducted by many organizations on the issue of political reform. The Chinese Academy of Social Sciences convened a discussion on April 28–29, 1986, on this topic. In June, a large conference was held in Taiyuan, bringing together central, provincial, and local political scientists.[6] In July, the Central Party School had extensive discussions, with participants from various agencies presenting papers with specific suggestions. Some people thought reform might come as early as fall 1986.[7] Wang Zhaoguo, head of the party secretariat, spoke at the party school's commencement on July 16, and advocated reforms that would improve the cadre system and expand the role of the people's congresses, democratic parties, and mass organizations.[8]

The top leadership had its annual July/August policy review meeting at the summer capital at the beach resort of Beidaihe. Some of those present with Deng Xiaoping were the General Secretary of the Chinese Communist Party Hu Yaobang, Premier Zhao Ziyang, and Hu Qili, all younger leaders and supporters of reform. In addition, there were President Li Xiannian, head of the Discipline Inspection Commission Chen Yun, and Peng Zhen. These senior leaders had extensive connections in the military and bureaucracy, and all were basically confident that the political and economic system they had created in the 1950's was sound in theory and needed only marginal improvements.[9] They discussed in some detail the question of reform of the political system. The reform momentum was broken when two top military men (Yang Shankun and Yu Qiuli) changed sides.[10] The conference did not endorse the need for urgent reform of the political system. Many senior leaders were rather cool towards the idea. Indeed, debate was reported to be "heated" and "endless." Hong Kong observers reported Chen Yun, among others, as being opposed to political reform.[11]

The conference agreed that the banner of human rights, democracy, and freedom should not be left in the hands of capitalism. These values should also be supported by socialism. They also accepted the idea that theoretical circles could be bold in making explorations and need not be confined to Marxism.

It also agreed to allow discussion about political structural reform, but also stipulated that the adoption of any concrete reform steps should be postponed. Any political structural reform had to retain the party's leadership, and that the four cardinal principles must not be abandoned. (These four cardinal principles are: 1) adherence to the socialist road, 2) the people's democratic dictatorship, 3) the leadership of the communist party, and 4) Marxism-Leninism and Mao Zedong thought.) Conference participants judged that China's current political system as a whole was basically suited to the needs of economic development. Only some aspects of this system were not suited or not completely suited to the needs of economic development.[12]

The Secretariat of the Chinese Communist Party set up a working group to study the issue of political reform. The group was headed by Hu Qili, and included Wang Zhaoguo, Zhu Houze (head of the party propaganda department), and Xiang Nan (former head of Fujian province). All were thought to be close to party head Hu Yaobang.[13]

At about this time, at the end of July, Vice Premier Wan Li spoke at a national symposium on soft sciences. He acknowledged that the country lacked adequate support systems for policy consultation, appraisal, supervision, and feedback.[14] His speech, published after the Beidaihe meetings, made clear that political issues could be discussed openly. He started off by referring favorably to the "One Hundred Flowers" policy of 1956, when intellectuals were encouraged to speak out critically:

In order to produce a democratic, egalitarian and consultative political atmosphere, we must firmly implement the policy of "let a hundred flowers bloom, and a hundred schools of thought contend." We must carry it out in the scientific and technological fields and in the literary and artistic fields. We must also carry it out in the spheres of policy analysis and decision analysis. We must implement the policy not only in the realm of the natural sciences, but also in the domain of social sciences. We must adhere to this strategic policy in the theoretical and cultural construction, and in our political life. It is an important symbol of a high degree of socialist democracy.

Continuing, Wan Li realized that China's intellectuals would not automatically be reassured by reference to this one hundred flowers policy. Historically, the one hundred flowers period was followed by the anti-rightist campaign, in which those who did criticize the government were attacked. Many were jailed, sent into internal exile, or found their careers blocked. Wan had to reassure intellectuals that the new period of debate would not have the same results:

Thirty years have passed since the policy was proposed. Yet, it is not being genuinely implemented. For a time, it was even used as the so-called struggle strategy of "lure snakes out of holes," which was most unfortunate. An important factor which accounts for the failure is that we used to take political problems as having anti-Party, anti-socialism, and counter-revolutionary motivations. This perspective has produced many serious side effects. If we don't change this perspective, we will still hold that only scholarly academic problems can be debated, while political ones cannot. But often, these two kinds of problems cannot be separated. Once something goes wrong, academic problems will become political ones, both to be treated with sticks. As a matter of fact, on many occasions, it is very difficult to separate academic problems from political ones. The play "Hai Rui Dismissed from Office," brought extreme adversity to the writer, comrade Wu Han.[15] Is it an academic problem or a political one? With policy and decision analysis, it is even more difficult to separate them. Sometimes, academic problems account for 30 percent of an issue, while political ones constitute 70 percent. Sometimes, academic problems account for 70 percent, while political ones are 30 percent. Therefore, separating them is not important. What is important is to carry out the aforementioned policy towards political problems and policy analysis itself.

For Wan Li, the key point was that political issues could now be discussed safely:

All the political and policy problems should be studied. They can be debated before decisions are made. Dissenting views must not be attacked from the higher plain of principle and in the context of a two-line struggle, as was done in the past . . .[16]

Intellectuals were reassured by Wan Li's words. They spoke and wrote more seriously about democracy. Most intellectuals heeded the requirement that discussion be limited to academic, theoretical perspectives. In November, this restraint was breached by a few. The student demonstrations of December, of course, shattered the distinction between academic discussion and political organizing.

Of course it was necessary to offer a theoretical foundation for democratic reforms in the scriptures of Marx and Lenin. One important Chinese writer, Wang Ruoshui, had been working on this challenge for many years. He had been a deputy editor of *People's Daily* until his removal in October 1983 for arguing that alienation was possible under socialism.[17] Party ideologue Hu Qiaomu attacked this. In 1986, Wang Ruoshui was able to publish domestically his views on humanist Marxism:

When speaking of Marxism, people first think of class struggle and the proletarian dictatorship....Because of this, Marxism was mantled with a color of harshness and cruelty...According to Marx, however, both class struggle and the proletarian dictatorship are methods rather than goals. Marx' goal is to achieve the emancipation of the proletariat and all mankind and to realize communism. His philosophy is closely connected with this goal. It is not only materialist but also humanist....Marx repeatedly said that the fundamental principle of a communist society is "the full and free development of each individual."[18]

Marx most certainly did not anticipate that socialism would have a political system dominated by an elite, disciplined party, with lifetime self-appointments.

Yan Jiaqi, Director of the Institute of Political Science of the Chinese Academy of Social Sciences, argued carefully that Marxism was not a complete ideology for China. It needed to be supplemented by other viewpoints:

Our Marxism has become a particularly closed ideological system....Many ideas in mathematics, chemistry, physics, politics, economics, and sociology in the world are scientific....It is not scientific to say that with the exception of Marxism, all those ideas have no value, and do not belong to science....Marxism is the science guiding our socialist modernization and reform today; however, there are other theories, doctrines, and ideas of other branches of science. All scientific theories, doctrines, and ideas are needed in our modernization.[19]

China's scholars even found democratic insights in Lenin. After a few years of wartime communism, Lenin saw the problems caused by over-centralization. He introduced the "New Economic Policy" which relaxed central economic planning and encouraged the development of a commodity economy with more market interactions.[20] Some Chinese scholars consider Lenin's New Economic Policy to have been a proper long-term strategy for the early stages of socialist development, and not a short-term emergency policy to cope with the peculiar problems after World War I and War Communism. Chinese scholars also are studying Bukharin's insights closely. In many ways, he opposed the extreme centralization of the Stalinist model.[21]

If the current Chinese interpretation is correct, that Marx and Lenin inherently supported democracy, what has happened for the past sixty years in the world socialist movement? Lenin established a centralized democratic dictatorship under party leadership. This system was made more rigid by Stalin, and became the normal definition of a Marxist government. The system was imposed on Eastern Europe, and was adopted by China. Some Chinese scholars replied bluntly: the world socialist movement since the 1920s has made a mistake.[22] It has not followed true principles of Marx and Lenin. This implied that China belatedly should make the correction.

## POLITICAL REFORM TO COMPLEMENT ECONOMIC REFORM

Why are people in China talking about political reform? The first reason is economic. Over the past decades economic policy generally followed the classic Soviet model. The government directly provided most of the investment funds and has directly or indirectly administered all economic enterprises, including factories, farms, and commerce. The state controlled interactions between enterprises through systems of material allocations and price setting. It eliminated a labor market by assigning life time jobs to school graduates. It also allocated housing. Black or gray markets and underground factories existed to some degree, so a few corners of the economy functioned semi-autonomously from the state. In general, politics have been virtually indistinguishable from economics. Economic enterprises were government offices.

State control over China's economy was not a new phenomenon introduced by communism. For thousands of years, the Chinese state had played a major role in managing and regulating the economy. It controlled irrigation and water works, much of industry, and commerce. China did not have a vigorous class of economic entrepreneurs independent of the government, as Europe did on the eve of its industrial revolution. The communist system of state control over the economy reinforced this old pattern, and did not create it.

During the first three decades of communist rule, the economic growth rate has been fairly high, although the investments and human costs were prodigious, and actual improvements in standard of living have been slow and uneven. Income growth in rural areas has been marginal in most regions. Serious pockets of poverty remained. In urban areas, housing and public transportation were crowded. Meats, cooking oils, and other foodstuffs were sometimes in short supply. Jobs were not available for all the high school graduates.[23]

The growth rate of China's economy was not as high as those of Hong Kong, Singapore, South Korea, and Taiwan, which relied on exporting to a world market. This comparison is not very useful, and in fact may be misleading, because a gigantic, continental economy such as China's simply cannot follow the same policy as a city–state or a small economy. The world market simply could not absorb all the shirts, sweaters, and transistor radios China could export. China followed a different strategy, and grew more rapidly than other large developing nations such as India or Pakistan. Efficiently or not, China's strategy and system did pull China out of its poor agrarian past into the middle stages of industrialization.

China has undergone a substantial industrial and technological revolution, and now has a reasonably advanced, diverse, sophisticated, complex economy.

Nevertheless, China is far from satisfied with its economic performance. Deng Xiaoping unfavorably compared China to global experience:

In 1980 our per capita GNP was only about US$250 and today it is just a little over US$400, which puts us behind 100 countries in the world. By the end of the century when we have become well off, the per capita GNP will only have reached US$800–1,000. . . . Even by the end of the century, we will still be working to eliminate poverty.[24]

The question now is the appropriate institutional arrangements to ensure that China grows at least this rapidly.

Economists inside and outside China argued that China's command economy had serious inefficiencies. China's leaders have accepted this analysis.[25] They decided to transform China's command economy into a "commodity economy," that would be shaped by market interactions. Starting in the late 1970's, China began experimenting with reforms in economic organizations.[26] In agricultural experiments in Sichuan and Anhui, responsibility for farming was contracted out to households and marketing was encouraged.[27] When this was coupled with higher farm prices, production and income soared. These policies spread very rapidly in the early 1980's. To insulate the rural economy from political factors, the system of the People's Commune, which had placed the rural economy under political direction, was dissolved. Separate local township governments and economic cooperatives were revived.

Reform of urban industry has been much more difficult.[28] Experiments with industrial reform began in Sichuan in 1978, and spread during the next years. A comprehensive urban reform program was announced by the Third Plenum of the 12th Central Committee on October 21, 1984.

The reform program rapidly ran into numerous problems. First, foreign trade was liberalized. Inefficiency, corruption, and an overvalued exchange rate resulted in enterprises importing consumer goods and then selling them domestically for profit. China's foreign exchange reserves plummeted. Import contracts were broken and trade relationships were disturbed. Monetary reforms led China's banks to extend credit recklessly in late 1984. Within a few months, banks were facing deficits, and China's financial system was upset, needing more adjustment.

Another set of problems emerged when the government started to implement price reforms. Food prices were allowed to rise, to reduce the large government subsidy caused by higher commodity prices to the farmers. Prices of other commodities and products went up to meet costs of production, to generate more profits, and to eliminate losses of production enterprises. Official reports put inflation at 22 percent in 1985 and 26 percent in 1986, and some people think it was more. Wage reforms fell short of the inflation rate for many people. Frustration brought on sporadic strikes and a soccer riot in Beijing.

The government proposed that enterprises have more independence, and pay taxes rather than turn over profits to the government. Many government administrators were reluctant to give up their accustomed pattern of public finance, or to cease the micro-management of production. Local officials invested in profitable local factories and hoarded inputs materials. This caused dislocations in the factories of the central government.

Shenzhen, the special economic zone near Hong Kong, began to experiment with reforms in the early 1980's. There was over-expansion of Chinese investment. Initial hopes for immediate foreign investment in export enterprises that would show a quick profit in foreign exchange were not met.

The initial attempts to reform urban industry showed that piecemeal reform was difficult. The fundamental problem was that the political system still controlled the economy and could make investment, production, personnel, and pricing decisions. Many foreign observers presumed that the communist bureaucracy would ultimately undermine the reform program, as had happened in previous reforms in other communist countries.

The Chinese leadership reached the same conclusion, and recognized that reform of the political structure was an integral element of economic reform. Economic enterprises could not engage in market behavior until bureaucratically imposed distortions and constraints were removed. Government had to shift its functions from managing the economy to providing the infrastructure that would enable markets to function better.[29]

Deng himself was very explicit about this in comments to a visiting Japanese politician on September 3, 1986:

The major problem is that the political structure does not meet the requirement of the reform of the economic structure. Therefore, without reforming the political structure, it will be impossible to safeguard the fruits of the economic reform or to guarantee its continued advance.[30]

Premier Zhao Ziyang commented while traveling in Yugoslavia:

With the overall unfolding of the economic structural reform, the functions of the government will also change; the government structure and the cadre system must be reformed in a step-by-step way. With no changes in this aspect, it will be impossible to suit the needs of the economic structural reform.[31]

Leading political scientists, including Yan Jiaqi and Wang Huning, echoed these insights.[32]

A political-economic system is somewhat like a giant machine. If one gear is changed with a new, improved design, then complementary changes must be made in the gears that mesh. Otherwise, the new, improved gear simply breaks the other parts, rendering the entire machine inoperative. In China's case, the argument went, new political gears were needed to mesh with new economic gears.

Whether agreeing or not with the market-oriented policy, orthodox Marxists had to accept the fact that China's very substantial economic growth and increasing diversification and sophistication required changes in the system of economic management. Marxist theory would require that a change in the economic foundation of society would require change in the political superstructure.

The party journal *Red Flag* was explicit about this reality:

The superstructure is determined by the economic base and in turn serves it. This is a basic Marxist viewpoint on the relationship between economy and politics. Political structural reforms and economic structural reforms depend on and dovetail with each other. Economic structural reforms cannot be successful unless political structural reforms are carried out. An important aspect of economic structural reform is to improve the state's methods of managing the national economy.[33]

## STRENGTHENING THE POLITICAL SYSTEM

A second reason for political reform was to maintain and strengthen its legitimacy. Several reasons made this urgently necessary.

The cultural revolution of the 1960s and 1970s very seriously undermined the legitimacy of the communist leadership. In Chinese minds, a chief responsibility of government is to prevent chaos. Incredibly, however, during the cultural revolution the communist leadership not only failed to prevent chaos leading to imprisonment, murder, devastated lives, and economic loss, it actually created chaos. Moreover, ideological and power struggles undermined the notion that the party was following a scientific ideology that was sure to lead to success. Ideology degenerated into slogans to support factions in the struggle. In this way, ideology ceased to provide legitimation to the regime. A major goal of Chinese political scientists has been to prevent the recurrence of another cultural revolution.

Corruption and mismanagement have further weakened the system. Moreover, as the economy expanded and international relations became more complex, the demands on government for fast decisions on complex technological and economic issues increased. At the same time, the ability of government leaders to make such decisions deteriorated.

Chinese political scientists have used strong language to underscore the urgency of reform.

In terms of long-term political stability, it can be said that the present political structure is incapable of guaranteeing that there will be no recurrence of serious disruption to socialist democracy and the legal system . . . in terms of the daily operation of the state mechanism, the present political structure is incapable of guaranteeing the effective and timely detection, exposure, punishment, and prevention of such corrupt phenomena as the abuse of power, the use of power for personal gain, and violation of law and discipline.[34]

The deterioration of political efficiency in the 1980s is a natural result of the historical processes of the communist revolution of 1949. That revolution created a distinctive political system and institutional culture that was not well adapted to the needs of a modernizing economy in the 1980s. The communist revolution brought into power a communist party with strong rural roots. Party leaders and members were brought up in a world of unquestioned patriarchal authority. The image of a good political system was a strong emperor who could impose order and unify China. Throughout the communist party, as in every other aspect of Chinese society, personal relations were crucial. Organizational patterns within the communist party resembled, to some extent, those in traditional Chinese secret societies. Superstition was far more prevalent than science. People sought a leader whom they could worship as a god.

It was also a world of violence. In the countryside, landlords sometimes enforced their power with violence, and peasants occasionally reacted in kind. Invasion by Japan called for armed resistance. The civil war between the National Party and the Communist Party also became bloody. In these wars the party naturally developed work styles for decision making and implementation that stressed secrecy, strict discipline, and decentralized action to support a central objective. Total acceptance of party discipline was necessary. There could never be public debate about party policy in the face of war.

After the revolution, guerrilla fighters became government bureaucrats, but they were still at war. In the 1950s they faced the Korean war on their borders. Persistent hostility from the United States, coupled with nuclear threats, contributed to a bunker mentality. Accepting the ideology of Marxism, their image of progress was a proletarian democratic dictatorship. They followed the model of the Soviet Union, which became an "elder brother." Tensions with the Soviet Union after 1960 reinforced the feeling of international tensions, but did not erode confidence in Marxist ideology.

Not surprisingly, China's leaders retained the work style of guerrilla fighters, even though the problems of social and economic development were very different. They also retained traditional ideas that the winner of a revolution gets power that can be translated into executive perks, banquets, and favors for friends and relatives. Indeed, the communist political system gave political leaders direct control over an expanding economy. This enlarged the opportunities for discretionary favoritism. Some leaders continued the previous traditions of "local emperors." Many cadres went to school to become literate, and to obtain technical training. They also had endless ideological training. Despite this training, such traditional ideas did not disappear quickly, especially when they could be rewarded by the economic environment.

In the years since the revolution, there has been little turnover of political leadership. (To be more precise, the turnover of the cultural revolution in the late 1960s was turned over again, so that the original leaders resumed their positions.) Even where there has been personnel turnover, the original revolutionaries established an institutional culture in which younger cadres had to function. They had to accept, learn, adopt, and excel in these traditional guerrilla modalities of behavior to be promoted by their superiors. In this manner, the work styles of the revolutionary period were institutionalized and continue, long after the revolution.

The revolution is now almost forty years old. Young guerrilla leaders who were in their twenties and thirties in 1949 are in their sixties and seventies now. China has changed a great deal. It is now a substantially industrialized country entering the "information age." Some of the traditionally oriented personnel and work styles are out of date.

This guerrilla-style political system has several serious weaknesses, each of which erodes the political legitimacy of the system. One broad problem is abuse of authority, including various forms of corruption. The facts that government operates in secrecy, that government has such control over the economy, and that personal networks are so strong—these facts make abuse of power hard to avoid. Moreover Chinese tradition about the importance of family and personal relations and obligations place additional temptations and pressures on officials to use public authority for private purposes. Top leaders are fully aware of the temptations for corruption and the damage it can cause to political legitimacy. The party and government have numerous agencies to investigate reports of corruption, often coming from anonymous tips in letters to government agencies or newspapers. Reports of Chinese government investigators provide rich material for China's writers. Occasional punishments have been very severe, including execution.

In 1986 there was much discussion about corrupt behavior of sons (or sons-in-law) of very high ranking officials. Six sons of high ranking Shanghai cadres were convicted of rape. Three of them, including the son of the Chairman of the Shanghai Municipal People's Congress Standing Committee, were executed.[35] If Hong Kong gossip is to be believed, the son-in-law of Marshal Ye Jianying, a superb concert pianist, was jailed for carrying drugs and trafficking in gold. The son of party ideologue Hu Qiaomu was accused by sixteen women of rape.[36] He was reportedly condemned to death, but the sentence was suspended.[37] Children of Peng Zhen, Chairman of the Standing Committee of the National People's Congress, and the daughters of navy commander Ye Fei and General Xiao Jinguang were also in trouble.[38] Of course there is always the possibility that attacks on sons or relatives of high ranking officials, mostly conservatives, may also reflect deep factional conflicts in addition to questions about abuse of power.

At a less dramatic but more significant level, there is a widespread perception that the children of cadres from high to low are getting the better jobs, and are moving into business. They seem to have the contacts to buy and sell scarce commodities. They become middlemen in international trade arrangements. They get rare government loans to start up businesses. They get highly prized first class train tickets. There may be nothing illegal about this; they just happen to be in the right place at the right time. But it contributes to an image of cronyism and abuse of power.[39]

Other cases involve simple embezzlement and bribery. A typical case was that of a county party secretary who embezzled funds, accepted bribes, forged work reports, and lived lavishly at public expense. His wife travelled with him at public expense. He was criticized and removed from office.

Liu Binyan, one of China's top writers and a major victim of the "anti-bourgeois liberalization campaign" of 1987, detailed the system of corruption in a county in Heilongjiang. The manager of a coal company was able to generate large amounts of discretionary funds by overcharging for coal. Through an elaborate network of relationships cemented by gifts, cash, and marriage alliances, she assumed great wealth and power. Her friends included most leaders of the county communist party, who therefore were reluctant to investigate her activities.[40]

In urban areas, one type of corruption involves housing construction and assignments. In one case, the city gas company demanded 2 percent of the apartments in new buildings in exchange for hooking up gas pipes. Several of these apartments were taken over by the company's party secretary.[41]

Another manifestation of political problems is the phenomenon of "local emperors." These are local officials who assume they have the absolute power of an emperor in their locality. They are above the law and use the violence of the legal system to maintain their privileges. For example, one local party official was upset that a traffic policeman and construction workers challenged his right to drive on a road that was under construction and officially closed. Afterwards, the official sent armed police to beat up the workers and the traffic policeman. The policeman was taken to the police station for interrogation.[42]

Another example was reported from rural Shanxi. The local power, party secretary and elected deputy to the National People's Congress, "claimed his bicycle bell had been stolen, and asked . . . the village public security committee to question 85 villagers. They illegally took 75 of them into custody and bound and beat some of them." He also embezzled public funds totaling 4,300 yuan. This person was eventually convicted and sentenced to four years imprisonment for illegal interrogation and custody.[43]

The history of the Chinese revolution left another legacy. A revolution is made by youth. When the Chinese revolution succeeded in 1949, a large group of people entered government service at about the same time and at about the same ages, 20–40 years old. They are aging simultaneously, are now aged 60–80, and are now retiring at the same time. This means that China must undergo a crucial generational change in leadership during this decade.

The older party leaders realize that they are not immortal, and that continuation of the communist party system requires new recruitment and new leaders. The issue is no longer whether China will have new leaders. Biology is enforcing that answer. The questions now are who these new leaders will be, how they will be selected, what will be the basis for their legitimacy, and in what institutional environment they will function. Deng has stressed this issue in his writings:

> . . . [W]e must take the long-term interest into account and solve the problem of the succession in leadership. [Older cadres'] primary task now is to help the Party organizations find worthy successors to work for our cause. This is a solemn duty. It is of great strategic importance for us to ensure the continuity and stability of the correct leadership of our Party and state by having younger comrades take the "front-line" posts while the older comrades give them the necessary advice and support.[44]

In selecting a new generation of leaders, however, nepotism is a serious risk, particularly in a system in which selections are made by consultation and appointment, and not by competitive elections. This issue became very important as the party systematically selected in 1985 the next generation of leaders, called "the third echelon."

New leaders have been appointed by the existing older generation. There has been a certain tendency for leaders to select their own children, in-laws, friends, or other relatives. Many city mayors and provincial leaders are sons or sons-in-law of the high-level cadres. For example, the governor of Guangdong, Ye Xuenping, is the son of Marshall Ye

Jianying.[45] Chen Yuan, assistant secretary of the Beijing party committee, is the son of Chen Yi. Deng Henggao, Chairman of the Scientific Commission of the Ministry of Defense, is the son-in-law of Field Marshall Nie Rongzhen.[46] Mutual agreements between senior cadres to promote each others' children have been alleged. These families are closely knit because there is a tendency for children of high ranking cadres to intermarry. Sometimes children are appointed or promoted as a way of acknowledging mistreatment of the father. In other cases, children are promoted as an inducement for the older generation to retire. Such practices are the subject of ridicule and undermine the reputation of the party. Some Chinese refer to the Communist Party as "the Princes' Party."[47]

In fact, the actual occurrence of these practices may be less than is commonly believed. The party has collected statistics showing that children of senior cadres at and above the vice ministerial level have been about 2–4 percent of positions at the provincial and ministerial level.[48] However, this does not include promotion of in-laws and friends pledged to help children.

Of course in some cases the children of leaders were good political leaders. They had political judgment and were trusted by many in the leadership. In many countries there is a tendency of children to follow their fathers' footsteps. This pattern is well established in politics and even more so in business. Nepotism in China is probably not especially extensive in comparison with international standards. An important distinction is the fact that in the West, children of politicians who seek elected office must still get voter approval, regardless of family background.

These various forms of abuse of authority are difficult to eliminate. A "connection network" is frequently set up, which involves a number of people inside and outside the party, who pursue "unhealthy" trends, abuse power, collaborate, and help each other pursue political and economic interests. Once established, such a connection network is resilient and hard to destroy.[49]

It is difficult to gauge the exact extent of this corruption, much less compare it with corruption in other countries. It could well be far less than in the Soviet Union, Poland, India, or the United States. However, even if corruption is less in China, it could have even greater negative political consequences. Many transactions that are considered corrupt in China would be normal business payments for services rendered in the United States. For example, consulting services, lobbying, finders' fees, brokers' payments, and so forth are not considered corruption in the United States. In contrast, in China, because virtually all business activities have taken place under the jurisdiction of party and government, the political implications of even small, "normal" payments can be far more serious than in the United States. They involve possible betrayal of public trust. In the United States, the government is insulated from much corruption by the fact that it is largely separated from market forces and business enterprises. Moreover, in the context of a capitalist ideology such as in the United States, personal gain is considered appropriate. In contrast, in China's socialist ideology of selflessness, any personal gain is suspect.

An opinion poll of 2,518 people in 23 cities revealed the top complaint was the abuse of power for personal gain by government and communist party officials. Control of corruption was judged to be urgently needed.[50] The party leadership understands that these patterns of administration seriously undermine the legitimacy of the whole political system. Su Shaozhi, the Director of the Institute of Study of Marxism, Leninism, and Mao Zedong Thought of the Chinese Academy of Social Sciences warned explicitly about this danger:

As it is, the public often talks about "unhealthy tendencies," which is the case when the cadres in the party and government and their children engage in business, and when officials are appointed in line with favoritism. These problems are all examples of special privileges, and privileges are deeply marked by feudalism. Such problems as engaging in trade and appointing people can never be considered a capitalist entrepreneurial spirit or a capitalist commodity relationship. They employ feudal remnants to undermine the national economy and to spoil the party's prestige.[51]

Another Chinese writer noted that corruption is widespread, and that reforms are needed:

Power corrupts; and absolute power corrupts absolutely. This has been fully proved in both ancient and modern history, in China and in foreign countries. The history of our party has also furnished us with distinct examples in this regard. To stop the possible emergence of corruption resulting from an over-concentration of power, we must adopt practical and effective measures, including organizational, mass and media supervision and other supervisory forms, to legalize and systematize the supervisory work. This is an important issue in the Chinese political system that must be resolved.[52]

Political reforms to eliminate or (more realistically) to reduce corruption to a tolerable level were needed to strengthen and stabilize the political system. At a broader level, the relaxation of state control over society would reduce the responsibility of political leaders for solving all problems. The political system could be stronger and more stable if its responsibilities were more limited. These were some objectives of the proposals for reform.

## CHINA'S GENERATION GAPS

The third pressure for political reform comes from China's younger generations. They demand more political freedom. Because of China's tumultuous history this century, each generation of Chinese has had very different experiences. These fundamentally different life experiences have resulted in different life outlooks, political cultures, and political experiences and demands. China's younger generations have not made a political compact with the Chinese Communist Party, as the older generations did in 1949. This presents important political problems for the system.

People who matured before the communist revolution (i.e., who were about 20 years old in 1949) are now approaching 60, or older. They were roughly 11 percent of the population in 1982.[53] They recall the problems of China before the revolution, including poverty, famine, invasion, civil war, and such horrors. The very maintenance of life was a major challenge, and could not be taken for granted. At the international level, China was the sick man of Asia, and extraterritoriality gave foreigners immense power. At the personal level, family control was intense, and marriages were arranged. From a political point of view, this older generation craved a government that could give peace and stability, that could set in motion sustained economic development, and could regain China's international position. Their demand was simply for an authoritarian system that was effective and enlightened, from a Confucian perspective. For most of the population, democracy was not only not a demand, it was not part of their conceptual framework. At best, it was a vague phrase that could be incorporated into slogans such as the Nationalist Party's "tutelary democracy," or Mao Zedong's "democratic dictatorship" with a "mass line."

Very few people in this generation had any real appreciation of Western democratic values. Some people had contact with the Western missionary movement in China. A few intellectuals and political activists went abroad to Japan or Europe. Within the original leadership of the communist movement, Zhou Enlai, Zhu De, and Deng Xiaoping were in Europe in the early 1920s. A very small number of Chinese intellectuals carefully studied and appreciated Western democratic values, but many who studied the West were favorably impressed by the dictatorial politics in Germany or the Soviet Union. Chiang Kai-shek, the leader of the Nationalist Party, spent time in Japan and absorbed an authoritarian perspective. He also visited the Soviet Union and learned Lenin's organizational principles there. As leader of the Nationalist Party in the 1930s, he had many advisors from Germany. Of those who understood Western democracy, many stayed abroad after 1949. Some of those who were in China were not trusted, but were criticized and neutralized politically.

China did have a small group of intellectuals who had a deep commitment to China's recovery as a nation, and to humanitarian values, broadly defined. Many of these were writers or in the performing arts after the May 4th Movement of 1919. At great personal cost, they have provided an enduring source of social criticism, both before the communist revolution and after.[54]

The vast majority of Chinese had no understanding of the West. What little knowledge they had led to hostility. The West was the source of imperialist invaders, cheap foreign goods that were destabilizing the economy, and ideas that were undermining Confucian harmony.

Throughout the period of Nationalist leadership, domestic unity was elusive, as warlord armies ruled different regions. China remained vulnerable to continued Japanese attack and expansion. Corruption was extensive. Flood, droughts, and famine periodically plagued vast rural areas. The Chinese gradually reached the conclusion that the revolutionary communist party, with its disciplined, austere, collectivist spirit, offered the only viable solution to reconstruct the country. In a broad sense, this generation made a political compact with the Chinese Communist Party.

China's next generation matured during the 1950s and early 1960s. They are now roughly aged 45–60, and constituted about 13 percent of the population in 1982. They grew up in a political environment that saw socialism as a solution to China's problems. The Soviet Union was the proper model of the future, and China's Communist Party, under the leadership of Mao Zedong, knew how to guide China into this future. To a large degree, the political demands of this generation were also limited. They accepted basic premises of communist leadership, and in general were satisfied to make their political input through informal consultation and discussion (the "mass line") within the party.[55]

The intellectual and political leaders of these two older generations suffered the brunt of the cultural revolution. They were criticized, humiliated, jailed, tortured, and murdered or goaded into suicide. These attacks generally had no sensible basis, and the victims had no recourse to due process.[56] Despite the intensity of cultural revolution, many victims survived and regained their prior positions.

Their experiences in the cultural revolution sensitized them to the need for law, due process, order, and institutional procedures to prevent such tragedies in the future. At the same time, many were left with a sense of bitterness and desire for revenge. They wanted to punish their former tormenters and to ensure power for themselves and/or their children.

The generation that matured during the cultural revolution (1966–

1976) is now approximately 30–45 years old. They constitute about 22 percent of the population. Their experiences were strikingly different from the generation before. One scholar argues that the structure of their high school experience was crucial in the formation of their culture. The limited opportunities for high school graduates coupled with the assignment of jobs by political leaders on the basis of very nebulous political virtue combined to create a high school environment of competition, distrust, and cynicism.[57]

During the cultural revolution, they were told that capitalist forces could, in theory, take over the Communist Party, and therefore it was not infallible. It might take China on the wrong road. They were sent for years of work in farms and factories throughout China. They traveled extensively. Their rich experiences gave them extensive training and a deep understanding of the realities of China. They were exposed to slogans such as "make revolution," and "swim against the tide," which gave them justification to think independently. They were taught and encouraged to attack their elders and supervisors. They discovered that for many leaders in localities and enterprises, the revolutionary slogans simply covered up power struggles, corruption, and abuse of authority. After Mao's death, this generation spearheaded the Democracy Movement of 1978–1981 and thereby showed its independence of thought, seriousness of purpose, and confidence in action. This generation is now struggling with the practical problems of life in China: career development, two-career families, inadequate housing, crowded buses, children in school. Their varied backgrounds give them confidence to become China's new entrepreneurs.[58] People of this generation are just now being promoted to positions of authority. In many cases they act in a very different way from their predecessors. They have the energy, experience, and confidence to be practical. It is this generation of leaders that will define future phases of political reform.

China's youngest adult generation has matured in the 1980s. They constitute a surprisingly large portion of the population, because of the high birth rates after the bad years of 1959–1961 and the cultural revolution. Those born between 1962 and 1971 constituted about 20 percent of the population in 1982. They were toddlers in the cultural revolution, and know it only second and third hand. They have matured with the political system telling them to excel in studies, to be open to the West, and to make money. Those with urban backgrounds have not been sent down to the countryside. Their political system has not guaranteed them a job, has encouraged them to establish their own businesses, and is now (after October 1, 1986) offering them only fixed-term contracts at factories or other locations. Today's college students, my students, the students who demonstrated in December 1986, come from this generation.

The difference between their experiences and their grandparents is vast. They know not about the chaos and famine of previous generations, but about the inability of the economy to grow as fast as their rising expectations. Not worried about the basic availability of food, they are concerned about equipping a house with refrigerator, television, stereo set, washing machine, and furniture, so that they can get married. They complain about air and water pollution.

They have not experienced the extraterritorial powers of foreigners in China, and do not think about China as the "sick man of Asia," being carved into a watermelon. Instead, they know about China's nuclear arsenal and space program. Western countries, including the United States, are models of successful, technologically advanced societies, not dangerous imperialist powers.

The young generation has a very different image of femininity now. Their vision is not the foot-bound lady of the past, not the child bride nor the Shanghai prostitute. Instead it is Olympic level women volleyball players, gymnasts, and basketball players. The new image of femininity became an issue in 1986. China debated whether to allow Chinese women to participate in international body-building competition. The problem was what to do about the bikini costume, which is the standard wear in international competition. Conservatives considered the two piece bathing suit too immodest. Reformers won, and Chinese women did compete (tastefully) in a demonstration contest that was broadcast on Chinese television.

Reading material for the younger generation includes (in recent translation) European Enlightenment authors (Locke, Montesquieu) writing about government being formed by social contract; Nietzsche's views that political leaders are men, not gods, and that citizens have the power to change politics; Freud's writings that sexuality is a normal, integral aspect of life; Fromm's writings on humanism; and writings of Thomas Paine and the speeches of Patrick Henry on the importance of liberty. They are familiar with Martin Luther King's dream of a world of freedom and justice, often used in China for English language instruction. My students were eager to read and discuss Western philosophy. One voracious student, determined to become an "American hand," had a plan to read systematically virtually all of Western philosophy. He may well succeed!

The different life experiences of this generation are now reflected in "modern" lifestyles, especially in urban areas. The obvious manifestations in China are roughly the same as elsewhere in the world: clothing, hair styles, music, art, concepts of leisure, new food tastes and (so far to a very limited degree) sexual values. Some dance disco to olympian standards. Not satisfied with having traditional Chinese holidays and communist holidays (Workers' Day, Army Day, etc.), they also want a holiday that is part of international and Western culture. They have appropriated Christmas Eve as a major holiday. The newly created Chinese Christmas is totally devoid of Christ, but has Christmas trees, Santa Clauses, and disco dance parties. The students have their own magazines and favorite writers from China, Hong Kong, Taiwan, and elsewhere. At Fudan a student-run "salon" featured high quality, imported coffee. Wall paintings, barely visible through the cigarette smoke, featured a reclining nude and isolated people drawn in grey.

From a political perspective, the urban, intellectual youth is very interested in Western-style democracy. After all, the West is the source of ideas about music, clothing, and economic progress. It is only natural that the political systems of the West should be considered also. For some, politics may not be so important. The first priority may be making money to buy new clothes. Others have intense political interests. China's young entrepreneurs, both in the private and public sector, vigorously support a stronger legal framework to reduce arbitrary government behavior, and to stabilize their business arrangements.[59]

Economically, they see a country of shortages for themselves. Perhaps most serious is the housing crisis. A 1986 survey revealed that 10.5 million urban families faced a housing shortage.[60] China has an urban population of about 240 million. If each household has an average of four people, then there are about 60 million urban households, of which roughly one-sixth face a problem. This shortage falls exactly on the young adults, seeking a private apartment so they can get married and start their own families. (Of course their parents suffer from this lack of privacy also.) One-third of urban households have no kitchen or running water, and two-thirds have no flush toilet.[61]

Urban public transportation systems are seriously overcrowded. Sardines would complain. At the same time, everyone knows that the privileged elite of the communist establishment can be assured of housing, official cars, and frequent banquet invitations.

Another set of frustrations lies in the job assignment system. A survey of scientists and technicians in Shanghai revealed discontent with their jobs. About 90 percent had asked for a job transfer and were denied. They have no opportunity for continued study or for sideline employment.[62]

In rural areas new patterns of consumption—clothing, motorcycles, lipstick, televisions, and so on—are already widespread. Western democratic values are probably less prevalent. Many traditional values are very strong, especially those dealing with marriage. This is clearly a transition period. Urban/rural economic exchange is increasing. The next decade could well bring new political values to the countryside.

What has the Communist Party done to merit the support of youth? Its major accomplishment in the last decade has been to criticize its own errors of previous decades. It has repudiated the cultural revolution, egalitarianism, and collectivism. The new policies may be better and more popular, but this is not the type of political history that creates enthusiastic legitimacy, as winning a revolution did in 1949.

The economic growth of the past nine years is impressive, and does create legitimacy. A massive housing construction program has been underway since 1980. Young people are optimistic that over the next five years the housing situation will be much improved if not solved, and they will obtain housing, get married, and start families. For this there is thanks. Road construction programs, construction of a subway in Shanghai, and other investments are being made in urban and inter-city public transportation systems. Nevertheless, as new housing is built farther from work sites, the demand on transportation facilities will probably expand as rapidly as the services.

Moreover, continued expansion of the economy at previous rates may be problematical. Ecological constraints will put new limits and costs on economic growth. World markets may be less receptive to China in the future. Also, at best, growth is inevitably somewhat uneven, and not everyone experiences economic progress for which to be thankful. Many resent the few who are successful.

Strengthening legitimacy through appeals to nationalism is a conventional political approach. Current policies toward Hong Kong and Taiwan seem adequately popular in China. As long as there are no major reversals, the government does not lose legitimacy. However, unexpected setbacks in this area could create domestic problems. Hong Kong's entrepreneurs may leave, undermining China's policy of absorbing an unchanged, affluent Hong Kong. In Taiwan, democratic reforms and the emergence of a new, independent political party create new question marks for the future. Taiwan's future leaders may have less reason to endorse the principle of unification than does the ruling Nationalist Party, with its social roots in the people who came from the mainland in 1949, and with its political legitimacy heretofore partially based on its claim to be the government of all China.

At present, the Chinese government bolsters its legitimacy with the constant stream of foreign dignitaries coming to Beijing to pay their respects, and by the impressive performances of Chinese athletes in international competition. These factors are positive but are not sufficient to justify the whole political system.

The occasional elections for indirect representatives do not strengthen legitimacy. The Communist Party nominates one candidate (or sometimes two) for each position. Generally, the nominee is a model worker who is pliant to the party's requests. He is not a real political representative. This type of electoral system does not create legitimacy for the Communist Party. It creates cynicism instead. Two postgraduates of the law department of Beijing University acknowledged, "At present, electing representatives is often like awarding an honorary title. Representatives are chosen as a reward for past behavior and achievement in work, not for what they can do politically."[63] Some people say that representatives usually do not debate policy but rather simply study party documents and instructions. Young generations see no reason why the party should not have to prove itself in some inter-party competition.

For these reasons, the generation gaps create legitimacy gaps. Older generations accepted the communist party as their liberators in 1949, but they could not commit China's next generation to make the same choice. China's youth have been born into a system of Communist Party rule; they did not select it. The Communist Party did not liberate today's youth from the semi-feudal, semi-colonial, chaotic past. From a youth perspective, the Communist Party is not a revolutionary party. On the contrary, it is the ruling establishment.

The younger generations have not made their own political compact with the Communist Party. They are open minded about politics, but are little moved by comparing today's China with the past. They look at other countries both in Europe and on the Pacific Rim in the present, and feel that China is not doing so well.

The problem is not caused simply or primarily by failure, incompetence, or corruption of the party and government, although such factors magnify the problem. Indeed, in many ways the Communist Party is quite effective. The problem is caused fundamentally by the fact that the political structure has no mechanism to renew automatically its legitimacy with each generation.

One could metaphorically say that China's youth have had an arranged childhood marriage to the Communist Party. The party wants now to consummate the marriage, but many young people would prefer to choose their own marriage partners. Whether the marriage is good or bad is irrelevant. Youth, particularly university students, would prefer to feel that they can make their own choices.

Of course this issue did not emerge overnight. The issue of political values of youth has been a serious concern to the communist leadership for decades. Much propaganda has been directed at youth since the 1960s. One dimension of the cultural revolution (1966–1976) was to reshape the consciousness of youth into firm supporters of party leadership. By the 1980s, the younger generations composed a substantial portion of the population, and their consciousness was more distinct.

Conservative octogenarian Peng Zhen recognized the fact that the different generations have different life experiences:

People under 50, however, do not have a clear idea. Our country was founded over 30 years ago. People who are 40 today were only a few years old when our country was founded. They have only a vague idea of how things were in those days. They may remember some things, but they were not actually involved. While some people between 40 and 50 may remember some things, some others do not. As for our college students today, who are in their 20s, they know nothing, or know very little, about the northern warlords or the oppressions of the three big mountains which burdened the backs of the Chinese people, or how the three big mountains were overturned.[64]

Chinese philosophers have summed up this generation gap. At a conference in late 1986, they acknowledged that the Marxist solutions of the earlier generation were no longer satisfactory:

[M]ost participants at the conference concluded that the existing philosophical system in this country is no longer suited to technological progress in the world and domestic modernization efforts. Existing philosophical books on Marxism have failed to reveal the entire paradigm of Marxism, participants argued. As a consequence, the works appear anachronistic and unappealing, a situation that philosopher Jia Chunfeng called a "crisis leading to a turning point."[65]

Given the fact that "the existing philosophical system" (Marxism, Leninism, Mao Zedong thought), provides the fundamental legitimation for the political system, this statement amounts to an admission of dissatisfaction with the political system from at least some portions of the population.

The depths of questioning in the ideological sphere can be seen in an observation by Su Shaozhi, Director of the Research Institute of Marxism, Leninism, and Mao Zedong Thought:

[N]o hard and fast line can be drawn between the socialist system and the capitalist system . . . Most of the basic contents proposed [in the capitalist democratic system] were progressive, such as the general election system, the system of power balance, democracy, human rights, and so on. We may carry these forward and make them tools for realizing the people's interests.[66]

The director of the propaganda department of the party's central committee (who was purged in January 1987) argued that Marxism-Leninism needed constant updating:

With basic Marxist viewpoints as our tools for understanding the world, we should keep up with all economic, cultural, and technological developments after Marx and Lenin and absorb everything useful—including those nuggets among the theories and cultures permeated by the prejudices of the exploiting classes. Only in this way can we keep Marxist theories forever dynamic.[67]

A disquieting harbinger of tension between students and government occurred in April 1986. Two students of history at prestigious Beijing University were arrested and charged with the very serious crime of counterrevolutionary offenses. Their crime? They had written and circulated an article exploring the theories of the young Marx.[68]

It must be emphasized that the different generation groups are in reality much more complex than outlined here. Especially among youth, there are many differences. Many of the youth appear to be concerned with developing their own careers, or finding ways of making money. Modernization means little more than new clothing, music, and dancing to many. In the rural areas, traditional ideas remain; the government rules and people obey, as long as government is reasonably effective and not too corrupt.

For many top political leaders, intellectuals, and students, there was strong interest in political reform in the summer and fall of 1987. They gave speeches and wrote article after article explaining the need for reform. The next chapter will specify the precise suggestions for reform that they made.

## NOTES

1. *Selected Works of Deng Xiaoping (1975–1982)* (Beijing: Foreign Languages Press, 1984), pp. 309–310. Published in China in 1983.

2. Roger Garside, *Coming Alive, China After Mao* (New York: McGraw-Hill, 1981).

3. Cheng Hsiang, "Tentative analysis of discussion concerning reform of the political structure," *Wen Wei Bao* (July 21, 1986); FBIS (July 24, 1986), p. W 1.

4. Ibid.

5. "Reforming political structure, strengthening legal sense," *Beijing Review*, no. 20 (May 18, 1987), pp. 14–15. Reportedly printed in the Chinese journal, *Organization and Personnel* (August 1986). Also cited in "Deng Xiaoping discusses political structural reform," *Da Gong Bao* (Aug. 8, 1986); FBIS (Aug. 8, 1986), p. W 9. "Deng Xiaoping criticizes Chen Yun at meeting," *Zheng Ming*, no. 108 (Oct. 1, 1986), pp. 8–12; FBIS (Oct. 9, 1986), p. K 10. Lo Ping, "Notes on a northern journey (2)," *Zheng Ming* (Oct. 1, 1986), pp. 10–12; FBIS (Oct. 9, 1986), p. K 10.

6. Xu Zhaoming, "The changing function of government," *Political Science Research*, no. 5 (1986), pp. 53–57. Available in Benedict Stavis (ed.), "Reform of China's political system," *Chinese Law and Government*, 20:1 (Spring 1987). Summarized by the same author in "Roundup on a theoretical forum on the function of the government," *Bright Daily* (July 28, 1986), p. 3; FBIS (Aug. 13, 1986), p. K 4.

7. "Discussion of Central Party School shows the focus of the reform of the political structure lies in the division of work between the party and government," *Ming Bao* (Aug. 12, 1986), p. 7; FBIS (Aug. 13, 1986), p. W 8.

8. "Wang Zhaoguo on political structural reform," *NCNA* (Aug. 31, 1986); FBIS (Sept. 7, 1986), pp. K 3–4. The full text of his address is available at *Red Flag*, no. 17 (Sept. 1986), pp. 6–15; FBIS (Sept. 22, 1986), pp. K 8–21.

9. "Planning for CPC Central Committee plenum begins," *South China Morning Post* (Aug. 7, 1986), p. 6; FBIS (Aug. 8, 1986), p. W 2.

10. Lo Bing, "The Huangpu Jiang roars on," *Zheng Ming*, no. 111 (Jan. 1, 1987); FBIS (Jan. 8, 1987), p. K 11.

11. Lo Ping, "Notes on a northern journey (2)," *Zheng Ming* (Oct. 1, 1986), pp. 10–12; FBIS (Oct. 9, 1986), p. K 10.

12. Cheng Hsiang, "News from Beidaihe," *Wen Wei Bao* (Aug. 8, 1986), p. 2; FBIS (Aug. 11, 1986), p. W 1.

13. David Chen, "CPC secretariat holds political reform meeting," *South China Morning Post* (Aug. 13, 1986), p. 16; FBIS (Aug. 13, 1986), p. W 5. Wen Chieh, "Beidaihe is brewing with activity," *Jing Bao*, no. 109 (Aug. 1986), pp. 86–87; FBIS (Aug. 20, 1986), p. K 11.

14. "Democracy essential to policy making," *Beijing Review*, no. 32 (Aug. 11, 1986), p. 5. An important publication of Wan Li's views in China was his speech "Making decision making more democratic and scientific is an important part of the reform of the political system," *People's Daily* (Aug. 15, 1986); see also note 16, below.

15. Criticism of this play was the initial salvo of the cultural revolution. Wu Han died during the cultural revolution.

16. "Making decision making more democratic and scientific is an important part of reform of the political system," *People's Daily* (Aug. 15, 1986). Available in Benedict Stavis (ed.), "Reform of China's political system," *Chinese Law and Government*, 20:1 (Spring 1987).

17. James Seymour, *China's Rights Annals no. 1* (Armonk, NY: Sharpe, 1985), pp. 125–136.

18. Wang Ruoshui, "On the Marxist philosophy of man," *Wenhui Bao*, (July 17, 18, 1986); FBIS (July 23, 1986), pp. K 7–13 (July 24, 1986), pp. K 1–8. Bill Brugger, "From 'Revisionism' to 'Alienation,' from Great Leap to 'Third Wave,' " *China Quarterly*, no. 108 (Dec. 1986), pp. 643–651.

19. Yan Jiaqi, "To develop, China must adopt an overall approach of cultural opening up," *Liaowang Overseas*, no. 40 (Oct. 6, 1986), p. 12; FBIS (Oct. 10, 1986), pp. K 5–7.

20. Chen Qiren, "Socialist theory, practice and commodity economy," *Shijie Jingji Wenhui*, no. 5 (1986), pp. 30–36.

21. Gao Ming, On Bukharin's theory of State Capitalism and the transition period. Fudan University, International Politics Department, MA essay, 1985.

22. Chen Qiren, "Socialist theory," p. 33.

23. Elizabeth Perry and Christine Wong, "Introduction: The political economy of reform in Post-Mao China: causes, content, and consequences," in Elizabeth Perry and Christine Wong, *The Political Economy of Reform in Post-Mao China* (Cambridge: Harvard Council on East Asian Studies, 1985), pp. 2–5.

24. "Deng on recent events in China," *Beijing Review*, no. 31 (March 30, 1987), p. 34.

25. Nicholas Lardy, *Agriculture in China's Modern Economic Development* (New York: Cambridge University Press, 1983). Hsueh Mu-ch'iao, *China's Socialist Economy* (Beijing: Foreign Languages Press, 1981).

26. Excellent reviews of the early efforts to reform are available in Stephen Feuchtwang and Athar Hussain (eds.), *The Chinese Economic Reforms* (London:

Croom Helm, 1983); Neville Maxwell and Bruce McFarlane, *China's Changed Road to Development* (New York: Pergamon, 1984); Perry and Wong, *Op. Cit.*

27. Introductions to rural reform include Jurgen Domes, "New policies in the communes: Notes on rural societal structure in China, 1976–81," *Journal of Asian Studies* 41:2 (Feb. 1982), pp. 253–268; Kathleen Hartford, "Socialist agriculture is dead: long live socialist agriculture! Organizational transformations in rural China," in Perry and Wong, *Op. Cit*; Andrew Watson, "New structures in the organization of Chinese agriculture: a variable model," *Pacific Affairs* 57:4 (Winter 1984–85), pp. 621–45; Vivienne Shue, "The fate of the commune," *Modern China* 10:3 (1984), pp. 259–283.

28. Surveys of industrial reform include Dorothy J. Solinger, "Industrial reform: decentralization, differentiation, and the difficulties," *Journal of International Affairs*, 39:2 (Winter, 1986), pp. 105–118; Susan Shirk, "The Politics of Industrial Reform," and Barry Naughton, "False starts and second wind: Financial reforms in China's industrial system," both in Perry and Wong, *Op. Cit.*, pp. 195–252; Zhang Gang, "How and why is economic reform failing," *China Spring Digest*, May/June 1987, pp. 3–19.

29. Bo Guili, "The function of local government in managing the economy, and the reform of local government institutions," *Political Science Research*, no. 3 (1986), pp. 42–45. Available in Benedict Stavis (ed.), "Reform of China's political system," *Chinese Law and Government*, 20:1 (Spring 1987).

30. "Not reforming the political structure will hamper the development of productive forces," *Beijing Review*, no. 20 (May 18, 1987), p. 15.

31. "Discussion of Central Party School shows the focus of the reform of the political structure lies in the division of work between the party and government," *Ming Bao* (Aug. 12, 1986); FBIS (Aug. 13, 1986), p. W 8.

32. Yan Jiaqi, "Our current political system and the goals of reform," *Liberation Daily* [Shanghai] (Aug. 13, 1986). Wang Huning, "Moving towards a political system with higher efficiency and more democracy," *World Economic Herald*, Shanghai (July 21, 1986). Both available in Benedict Stavis (ed.), "Reform of China's political system," *Chinese Law and Government*, 20:1 (Spring 1987).

33. "It is necessary to study how to further reform the political structure," *Red Flag*, no. 15 (Aug. 1, 1986), p. 2; FBIS (Aug. 13, 1986), p. K 3.

34. Li, "China's political restructuring . . . ," p. 18.

35. "Shanghai executes rapists," *Beijing Review*, no. 9 (March 3, 1986), pp. 5–6.

36. Lo Ping, "Two shocking major cases," *Zheng Ming* (July 1, 1986), p. 6–7; FBIS (July 10, 1986), pp. W 1–3.

37. Lo Ping, "Notes on a northern journey—Deng Xiaoping criticizes Chen Yun at meeting," *Zheng Ming*, no. 108 (Oct. 1, 1986), pp. 8–12; FBIS (Oct. 9, 1986), p. K 15. Terry Cheng, "Crackdown on senior cadre children slows," *South China Morning Post* (Aug. 6, 1986), p. 7; FBIS (Aug. 8, 1986), p. W 3.

38. Liang Heng and Judith Shapiro, *After the Nightmare* (New York: Knopf, 1986), pp. 139–47.

39. "Party embezzler fired," *China Daily* (Nov. 10, 1986), p. 3.

40. Liu Binyan, "People or Monsters," in Perry Link (ed.), *People or Monsters and other Stories* (Bloomington: Indiana University Press, 1983).

41. "Standards adopted after probe of building industry," *China Daily* (Dec. 16, 1986).

42. "Abuse of power investigated," *China Daily* (Dec. 1, 1986), p. 3.

43. "Illegal custody," *China Daily* (Nov. 17, 1986), p. 3.

44. "On the reform of the system of party and state leadership," in *Selected Works of Deng Xiaoping (1975–1982)*, (Beijing: Foreign Languages Press, 1984), p. 303.

45. *KYODO* (Oct. 16, 1986); FBIS (Oct. 16, 1986), p. K 1.

46. Dong Husheng, "Li Peng and the Soviet Connection," *China Spring Digest* (Jan./Feb. 1987), p. 10.

47. Lo Ping, "Chen Yun capitalizes on Hu Yaobang and Zhao Ziyang's vulnerable point," *Zheng Ming*, no. 99 (Jan. 1, 1986), pp. 6–8; FBIS (Jan. 6, 1986), pp. W 3–8.

48. Chang Hsing, "Princes' party?" *Ming Pao* (Dec. 30, 1985), p. 5; FBIS (Dec. 31, 1985), p. W 1.

49. "Eliminate the connection network," *People's Daily* (Dec. 10, 1986), p. 1; FBIS (Dec. 18, 1986), p. K 16.

50. "Poll shows majority of people favor reform," *NCNA* (Aug. 27, 1987); FBIS (Aug. 28, 1986); p. K 23.

51. Su Shaozhi, "The precondition for reform of political institutions is getting rid of feudal pernicious influences," *People's Daily* (Aug. 15, 1986). Available in Benedict Stavis (ed.), "Reform of China's political system," *Chinese Law and Government*, 20:1 (Spring 1987).

52. Hu Ping, "Reflections on making policies democratically and scientifically," *People's Daily* (Dec. 8, 1986), p. 5; FBIS (Dec. 17, 1986), p. K 1.

53. Based on 10 percent sample of 1982 census. *Tongji nianjian, 1984* (Statistical Yearbook), p. 97.

54. Merle Goldman, *China's Intellectuals: Advise and Dissent* (Cambridge, MA: Harvard University Press, 1981).

55. John Lewis, *Leadership in Communist China* (Ithaca: Cornell University Press, 1963).

56. Anne Thurston, *Enemies of the People* (New York: Knopf, 1986).

57. Susan Shirk, *Competitive Comrades* (Berkeley: University of California Press, 1982).

58. Judith Shapiro and Liang Heng, "China: How much freedom?" *New York Review of Books* 32:6 (Oct. 24, 1985), pp. 14–16.

59. My impressions agree with Stanley Rosen, "Prosperity, privatization, and China's youth," *Problems of Communism* 34:2 (March-April 1985), pp. 1–29.

60. "Poor housing still plagues millions—survey," *China Daily* (Dec. 3, 1986), p. 1.

61. "Poor housing still plagues millions."

62. "Tapping scientists' potential," *China Daily* (Dec. 8, 1986), p. 4.

63. "Political democracy must be ensured," *China Daily* (Nov. 24, 1986), p. 4.

64. Peng Zhen, "The four cardinal principles are the guiding thought of the constitution," speech to the 19th meeting of the 6th NPC Standing Committee, Jan. 21, 1987, Central TV. FBIS (Jan. 27, 1987), p. K 17.

65. Zhang Xiaogang, "Philosophers probe forbidden zones," *China Daily* (Oct. 8, 1986), p. 4.

66. Kung Shuang-yin, "Director of the Research Institute of Marxism, Leninism, Mao Zedong Thought under the Academy of Social Sciences of China on political reform," *Da Gong Bao* (Sept. 17, 1986); FBIS (Sept. 29, 1986), p. K 16.

67. Zhu Houze, Excerpts of speech, July 1987. *China Daily* (Aug. 11, 1986), p. 4.

68. *Hong Kong Standard* (Aug. 21, 1986), p. 3; FBIS (Aug. 21, 1986), p. K 23.

# 2

## *Policies of Reform*

After 1978 serious discussions started on economic problems and potential reforms. Experimental reforms gradually broadened over the
1978–1986 period. By fall 1986, a comprehensive program was planned
for radical reforms in the economy and for gradual reforms in the
political system. This chapter will summarize the plans for reforms. The
next chapter will review the opposition to reform.

The broad strategy of reform emphasized division of power to reduce
centralization of authority in both the economic and political systems:

The key (or the breakthrough point) of democratic construction is to solve the
problem of over-centralized power, which leads to personal arbitrary action,
dictatorship, and makes a democratic system nothing but a form. How can we
resolve or decentralize the over-centralized power? The main way is through
division of power. There are two ways to do this job: one is to divide the power
in a vertical direction; the other is to divide the power in a horizontal direction.
In reforms of the economic system, we are emphasizing the former method. In
reforms of the political system, we are now, or we will begin to work, mainly on
the latter. It has been proven that dividing power in a horizontal direction is
more difficult to do than dividing power in a vertical direction.... [1]

The institutional forms to achieve division of power were not clear.
China's reformers had no pre-existing, concrete model of suitable reform
in a country that had a communist political system. The Soviet Union
provided the model for China, beginning in 1949. By the mid–1950s,
China was aware of the problems of this highly centralized Leninist-
Stalinist system. Since the late 1950s China has been trying to create an
alternative model. There has been no obvious, simple way of blending

Western democratic values with the four cardinal principles of the Chinese political system (the socialist road, people's democratic dictatorship, Communist Party leadership, and Marxism-Leninism, Mao Zedong thought). In particular, opening up the political system to competition without questioning the leadership of the Communist Party presented a deep dilemma. An article in the *Heilongjiang Daily* outlined the challenge Chinese reformers faced: "There is no ready experience available for reference in developing a form of socialism with Chinese characteristics. All we can do is to sum up continually the experiences gained in practice and proceed gradually."[2]

In the 1980s, many ideas and slogans of reform admittedly came from Western bourgeois history. One writer argued:

Indeed, it was bourgeois thinkers who first raised the slogans of "democracy, liberty, and human rights."... Whether we admit it or not, the many democratic institutions of our republic, such as universal suffrage and the constitution, are the outstanding outcome of what we have learned and absorbed from our predecessors.... Marx and Engels believed that when the time came, everybody could freely develop in an all-round way... In my view, therefore, we must make a concrete analysis of the political slogans of the bourgeoisie and should not oppose whatever the bourgeoisie advocate... We now raise the slogan of democracy, liberty, humanitarianism and give them a certain status because this is the need of the four modernizations program and the development of the reform.[3]

Nevertheless, it must be emphasized that the Chinese concept of democracy is not completely congruent with Western definitions. The Chinese phrase for democracy is *minzhu*, meaning "people's rule." The phrase is vague, and has a sense of broad participation and fairness. It does not necessarily imply anything about electoral competition, two/or multi–party system, legal rights, civil rights and liberties, or protection of minorities. In Chinese political culture, the concept of democracy includes the idea of strengthening the government, so the state can protect the people and build the national economy. In this regard, Chinese ideas of democracy are quite contradictory to traditional Western ideas. In the West, democracy has meant restricting the government so it can not interfere with the rising bourgeoisie. Democracy did not mean strengthening the government.[4]

## ECONOMIC MANAGEMENT

During 1986, China continued to push the economic reforms that had been underway since about 1980.[5]

Shenzhen, the special economic zone near Hong Kong, began experimenting with a system that was virtually free enterprise, at least for some enterprises. Entrepreneurs were urged to come to Shenzhen and invest, hire labor, and begin production. They were able to be completely independent of the normal government ministries.[6]

The rest of the country could not make this change all at once. A step by step approach was needed. The first step was to end the policy that all enterprise profits went to the government, and that higher levels of the government made all decisions for an enterprise. The new policy allowed factories to retain a certain portion of their profits. When profits exceeded targets, the extra profits could be kept at the enterprise and used for reinvestment and depreciation, wage bonuses, and welfare (including investment in housing). Likewise, if actual profits were lower than targets, wages could be diminished. This change in management began to give the enterprise some autonomy. This type of reform has already been widely adopted.

A related interim reform was to have the "director responsibility system," in which the director of an enterprise had sole authority and responsibility for production planning. This approach reduced interference in management by the party and government. It also improved decision making. Previously, under a committee system, anyone in the committee could block a decision by calling for "more discussion." In practice, the committee responsibility system meant that no one was responsible or accountable.[7]

More autonomy was accomplished when enterprises were reorganized into economically independent companies, responsible for their own income and expenses. They were not supported from the government budget. This policy was enforced in a wide range of enterprises, including many factories, restaurants, hotels, construction and transportation companies, and cultural activities (such as theaters). In large scale manufacturing enterprises, it is still considered experimental.

Some critics have argued that such a change was just a change in the name on the signboard of a unit; its personnel and activities remained unchanged. Although personnel was the same, the change to an independent economic enterprise required a different work style. The unit had to consider market needs and economic profitability of its activities. These requirements resulted in new behavior of the old staff.

For this change to be implemented thoroughly, a new law was needed, namely a bankruptcy law. China allowed a handful of enterprises to go bankrupt, on an experimental basis. These experiences were widely reported. The goal was to leave no doubt that an enterprise, including its workers and managers, faced dire financial consequences if it was managed badly. A top level Chinese study group visited Hungary and Yugoslavia, and quoted a Hungarian cabinet minister approvingly: "Without a bankruptcy law, the basic conditions of a market economy won't exist."[8] Bankruptcy law was discussed by the National People's Council at its 17th session in August 1986, but not passed due to widespread opposition. This was an unprecedented demonstration of independence by the NPC.[9] If unprofitable firms were to face the threat of bankruptcy, all firms should be competing on a level playing field. Prices had to be rational and subsidies had to be removed to assure that no firm had an unfair advantage.[10] The law was finally passed in December 1986.[11] A large scale social survey (the sampling frame of which is not very clear) showed that 91.6 percent agreed that heavily debt-ridden enterprises that are unable to pay back their debts should go bankrupt.[12]

Shifting from a planned, controlled economy to a commodity, market economy required a new role for banks. In the past, the banking system had been part of the system of economic controls. Banks did not make disbursements from an account until they had ascertained that the withdrawal was for purposes consistent with economic plans and state policies. Banks could take funds from accounts if they judged it necessary. For example, banks could serve as police and judge, and pay fines from a unit's account.

Starting in 1983, as China moved into a commodity economy, the function and scope of banking work began to change. More and more people and units were having more active bank accounts, so the workload of the banks increased. Also, as enterprises became more independent from state control, the bank's responsibilities began to shift away from bureaucratic control and toward providing services to the depositors.[13] Banks began to make investment loans according to economic criteria; they also monitored economic activities in the context of collecting loan payments.

Another economic lever is the introduction of a taxation system. Previously, government finance had been based largely on remittance of total profits of every enterprise. This meant that the government had to be involved directly in all aspects of enterprise management, as anything could affect profit and losses of state revenue. A simple tax could vastly reduce the government's direct involvement in micro-management. Of course there would still be room for bureaucratic arbitrariness in tax matters, and both domestic and foreign businessmen are quick to point this out.

China also began to develop a personal income tax.[14] Previously, state revenues came from profits and taxes built into the sale price of goods. An income tax has the advantage that it can produce state revenues without being directly related to enterprise management issues. The tax was being phased in for people with very high income levels. (Some of my salary as a foreign expert was withheld for taxes, but I was saved the burden of filling out complicated forms.) As incomes increase over the years, more people would pay this tax, and its revenue would rise. An income tax, of course, can also be used to redistribute income from wealthy to poor, and thereby serve some socialist goals of income equality.

The underlying theoretical reason in the past for direct government involvement in enterprise management has been that in accordance with socialist principles, the investment came from the government, and ownership was vested in the "whole people." The government managed things for "the whole people."

One of the most significant policies to break the reform impasse involved the ownership system.[15] In rural areas since the early 1980s, farmers were given (or sold or rented) rights to use farmland. Technically, they did not have actual ownership rights to the land. In urban and industrial areas, capital shares are being issued, to dilute the government's monopoly of ownership. Some cities began to set up limited stock markets. Another approach has been to lease or sell enterprises to individuals, so they can be managed independently from the government. In Beijing, state-owned department stores, small food shops, and medium-sized grocery stores have been leased and auctioned off to self-employed traders.[16] Prices for some shops have been 60–85 thousand yuan.[17] In Wuhan a large engine factory was leased to a group of workers. Similar steps have been taken in Shanghai, Shenyang, and other cities.[18] In Beijing, some state-owned enterprises will be reorganized into joint stock firms, and shares will be sold to the public. The state plans to retain a 51 percent share.[19]

This program was controversial. One writer warned that in practice very few people would be interested or able to purchase shares. Moreover, he felt that the state did have a proper function in enterprise management, to ensure efficiency. He urged that the state appoint trustees to manage state property, rather than turn property over to private managers or owners.[20]

Despite such reservations, private enterprise has been allowed. By the end of 1986 there were thought to be almost 20 million self-employed businessmen in China. They included tailors, restauranteurs, taxi cab owners, traders, carpenters, bicycle repairmen, consultants in trade and social science, medical doctors, and others.[21] They had an output value of about 10 billion yuan in 1986. In the previous five years, private businesses paid 7.8 billion yuan in taxes to the state.

China's new small businesses were especially concerned about government interference in their activities. Local governments have restricted private street vendors, have overcharged taxes, and have insisted on collecting irrational fines. In some places such problems have resulted in a sharp decline of the number of private traders.[22] The status of these private businesses was underscored by the First National Meeting of Self-Employed Workers in Beijing at the end of 1986. The meeting urged new laws to guarantee the legal status of private enterprise.[23]

Symbolic of the role of private business is a shift in the definition of social leadership. In the past the hero was the party leader who could mobilize people for some activity, or the military person willing to make great personal sacrifice. The new hero became the entrepreneur (*qiye jia*) who mobilizes economic resources to produce and market new things. He was the risk-taker—both economic and political risks. He could function in either the public sector or private sector. He served as a counterbalance against the bureaucracy. Entrepreneurs deserved more rewards, according to some commentators. "Chinese entrepreneurs as a whole, however, are not enjoying affluence proportionate to the hazards they take, and power in keeping their jobs and positions."[24]

Other crucial reforms were to create a labor market.[25] In the old system, the government assigned people to jobs, which were permanent. The difference from serfdom or caste was that assignments were not necessarily based on birth, although in the industrial sector, a child could inherit a position in the work unit of the father. This did not necessarily lead to work assignments that took best advantage of people's capabilities or interests. Personal jealousies could force bright younger workers to subdue their energies, for fear of outshining their superiors. A writer in *Economic Daily* observed:

Once a person is assigned to a work unit, he or she will probably stay there permanently. People cannot leave if their work units will not release their files. There is no environment in which people can fully display their initiative and competence. This rigid system has enabled jealousy to succeed in 'killing' people.[26]

Another commentator used very strong language to criticize the old system:

The job security system of ours has degenerated into a protective umbrella of the lazy and incompetent and an insurmountable obstacle to the capable and diligent. Either way it has become seriously detrimental to our social progress.

A drastic reform nothing short of revolution is overdue for the old personnel system. In a truly democratic socialist society everyone should have his or her rights and responsibilities clearly outlined and guaranteed.[27]

A survey revealed that 60 percent of workers were willing or strongly willing to change jobs. Only 20 percent indicated they were unwilling or reluctant to change jobs. Over 70 percent said they would prefer to choose their own jobs rather than to be assigned by the state and fixed to a work unit for their entire lives.[28]

The system of state appointments had two, contradictory political consequences. First, it assured control over young people in school. They acted in a disciplined way because job assignments were very much affected by the perception of party officials. However, from a political perspective, it left the government responsible for frustrations and inefficiencies resulting from this system.

There already have been some important reforms in the labor market. High schools and many local colleges ended compulsory job assignments. School graduates had to look for their own jobs. Many did not succeed, and were happy when the government finally assigned them a permanent job. In most top-ranked national universities, students still receive compulsory job assignments. This was judged necessary to assure that college graduates do not all stay in a few big cities but that they return to their original provinces and regions. Beijing's Qinghua University and Shanghai's Jiaotong (Communications) university allowed graduates to seek their own jobs in 1985. Altogether, the government assigned work for 24 percent of university graduates in 1985, and 69 percent of the graduate class of 1986.[29] These changes in the job assignment system meant that recent school graduates already were living in a different institutional environment than their parents, or even their older siblings.

A related policy innovation was to encourage foreign businesses to invest in China and to establish joint enterprises. The joint enterprises were, in theory, substantially outside the realm of direct government control. Special regulations were announced on October 11, 1986, explicitly affirming the autonomy of joint ventures.[30] Joint ventures provided an arena in which China could experiment with and learn about new management techniques. Foreign businessmen were quick to complain to the government about bad conditions, and they had a powerful threat: they could cease to do business and quickly undermine the policy of attracting more foreign capital.

The conversion of government offices to economic enterprises was a complex transition. The personnel are the same but they had to learn new roles. Bureaucratic relations and alliances are less important. Market needs, efficient management, and profits are new requirements. A change of this magnitude naturally will require several years, and many mistakes will be made along the way.

## SEPARATION OF PARTY AND GOVERNMENT

Many reformers argued that a crucial first step in reform was to change the role of the Communist Party in both the economic and political systems. Deng himself endorsed this view in comments to the Central Financial and Economic Leading Group on September 13, 1986:

The substance of reform should primarily be separating the party from government administration, finding a solution to how the party should exercise leadership, and how to improve leadership.[31]

The party's image was tarnished by too much involvement in day-to-day affairs. "Party leadership will actually be weakened if the party intervenes too much and without success," cautioned the party's theoretical journal.[32] To ensure that party branches could not interfere in reforms some party theorists even suggested dissolving the two million basic party branches.[33]

In economic enterprises, in the past, the party branch had a dominant role in the enterprise. It had to approve all enterprise decisions. In 1986 there seemed to be agreement on a reform that would separate the party from direct administration, and give the factory manager complete authority to make decisions and complete responsibility for his decisions. The director was given full responsibility for personnel appointments and decisions on rewards and punishments. The party had a more limited role of helping to inform workers of new policies.[34] Tests of this experimental policy were set up in several cities.

In January 1987 the government officially issued three sets of regulations to enforce this new system. The regulations included a 40 article regulation on the role of the enterprise director, a 31 point regulation on the responsibilities of the party organization, and a 20 article regulation on workers' congresses, to assure more democracy. (The workers' congresses were told to help the director and to accept the party's ideological and political leadership.)[35]

It was not a simple matter to change the personal and power relations in an enterprise suddenly. It was especially difficult to separate party and government at the individual enterprise when higher levels of administration did not make this separation. The actual implementation of this reform will be a crucial indicator that reforms are in fact being carried out.

A much more complicated matter was to separate the work of the party and government within the political system. Zhang Youyu, an eminent jurist and chairman of the China Law Association and the Chinese Political Science Association, highlighted the significance of this reform:

I think now we should begin with the separation of party and government. This principle was already determined by the central committee of our party.... The present problem is that there is no realistic practice. Comrade Deng Xiaoping said that the separation of the party and government should begin in the central committee. This is absolutely right.... The separation of party and government will only strengthen the leadership of the party, not weaken or abolish it....[36]

An article in *World Economic Herald* agreed:

The heart of reform is to solve the problem of the "party replacing administration."... This means that the party committee not only did the work of government, but also replaced the state organization.... Therefore, one of the short-term targets of the reform is not only to separate the party from the government.

The party must be distinguished from state power and from the executive organs of state power.[37]

While theorists urged the separation of the work of party and government, actual agreement and implementation on this point was not clear. Some conservatives argued that even if there were separation at the lower levels, the party–government combination at top levels had to be retained.[38] The shift of Zhao Ziyang from being premier of the government to being general secretary of the party in January 1987 did not reinforce the idea of separation of party and government.

## REFORM OF THE CADRE SYSTEM

Another major point in political reform has been to change the practice of permanent, life-long jobs for leaders and low level functionaries in the party and government (cadres). Deng Xiaoping's 1980 report focused on this, and U.S. political scientists have identified the crucial nature of this feature of the Chinese political system. Elderly cadres cling to their posts, to keep their honor and executive perks. They have no regular, graceful way to "exit." This blocks the regular infusion of younger people, with new ideas and work styles, into higher administrative levels.[39]

The key element in this policy was to induce old cadres to retire. Deng has been quite successful in getting retirements and making replacements at the top levels of the government since the late 1970s. In 1982 and 1984, substantial changes were made in personnel in the bureaucracy. Between 1983 and 1985, almost 90 percent of provincial leaders changed. In September 1985, 131 senior leaders resigned from the Politburo, Central Committee, Central Advisory Commission, and Central Discipline Inspection Commission. The new appointments were younger and better educated. It was the largest peaceful turnover of leadership that the People's Republic has seen.[40]

In Shanghai, new regulations specified that cadres must retire at age 60 (55 for women), unless there was some pressing reason for them to stay in office. In practice, most cadres eligible for retirement have in fact retired. This is part of a national policy. At age 58, cadres received compulsory retirement registration forms. Many cadres were unhappy about forced retirement because they wanted to continue working and receiving the privileges of office.[41]

To mollify them, the retirement program included many special, important benefits for cadres whose service to the revolution began before 1949. For them, pensions were above previous salaries. The Old Cadres Bureau provided automobile service, telephone, and assured adequate living space, so retirees suffered no loss of executive perks. More important, these retired cadre continued to have access to secret documents, reports, and meetings, and were asked to be consultants for various departments. Their political status was retained. Because the old cadres technically were on leave, and not retired, and because they remained on the official list of cadres, they were not permitted to seek new employment in the private sector.

The generosity of this program should be contrasted with the way officials were thrown out of office during the cultural revolution. They were shamed, beaten, imprisoned, denied medical care, and worse. The government considered the program of generous retirement benefits to be important in maintaining the political support of the old cadres for the policies of economic development, openness, and democratization. If China is ever to develop a regularized system of political mobility, it certainly is important to reduce the stakes of losing political power. Struggle for office will be much more relaxed if the consequences of loss are to retire in this graceful manner. Cadres who joined the revolution after 1949 had a less generous retirement package, more like those of regular factory workers.

By 1985 the program of retiring the older cadres and bringing in younger ones had been partially implemented. At the provincial level, during the 1981–1985 period, the percentage of leaders under 55 increased from 15 to 48 percent. The percentage of college educated cadres increased from 20 to 60 percent.[42]

For cadres who are not yet of retirement age, China was experimenting with procedures for identifying those whose work performance was inadequate, and who should be transferred, demoted, or fired. In one experiment tested in some departments, party and government officials at and above county level were assessed by their direct subordinates and leaders of subordinate units through an annual secret ballot. Those who failed to win the confidence of a majority were to be examined by higher authorities, who would decide whether they should be demoted or transferred. This approach was advocated to create a more competitive environment.[43]

Another aspect of the reform of the cadre system was to end nepotism. It was made clear that hereditary appointments violated communist policy. For example in Shaanxi, the Provincial Party Committee changed the positions of some cadres to prevent the formation of "interest groups through family ties." It was still recognized that "favoritism is still a serious problem that is hard to solve because it is a vestige of feudalism, that dies hard."[44]

What criteria should be used in selecting the new generation of leaders, the so called "third echelon"? Because China is stressing technical development, some recommend that leaders should have a strong technical background. Vice Premier Li Peng, adopted son of Zhou Enlai and trained in engineering in the Soviet Union, could be seen as a prototype of a new technocratic leadership. Hu Qili, another potential leader, has a technical background in engineering and factory management. Others fear, however, that the technocrats will stress centralized decision making, and may have little use for participatory politics or law.

Procedures were established for selecting the third echelon. First, candidates had to be chosen at their workplace, usually by secret ballot. Second, their colleagues were canvassed for opinions. Third, the personnel department checked a nominee's work and personal qualities. Finally, the party committee decided. Even stricter rules were applied to children of top party and government leaders. Promotion at or above the county level had to be reviewed by the central committee's organization department and approved by the secretariat.[45]

Hong Kong analysts speculated that there was controversy in China about this "echelon system." Reformers may have been upset at the rapid promotions given to young military leaders. The conservatives were presumed upset as Hu Yaobang's former associates of the Communist Youth League were selected into the third echelon.[46]

So far there has been discussion about, but not many examples of, selecting government officials through competitive elections. One experiment made a nod in that direction. Guangdong used public polls and secret ballots to determine if officials were excellent, qualified, or unqualified. Power to make decisions was retained by the organization department of the party committee, so actual power to make decisions was not entrusted to an electoral process.[47]

Some scholars in China are recognizing that in the future there should be more than one method for selecting cadres. Some leaders should be elected. Some can be appointed by higher levels as regular civil servants. Both political criteria and performance on entrance examinations can be used for making different types of appointments. Some might be hired on a fixed term contract.

Cadres naturally will resist any genuine competitive system of cadre selection, which involves the real possibility of losing a position. A precondition for this will be the creation of attractive alternative careers for cadres who lose elections or who are otherwise relieved of their posts. The increasing flexibility in the economy, including "specialized households" in the rural sector and new opportunities for entrepreneurship in the urban economy, begins to satisfy this need.

## STRENGTHENING THE LEGAL SYSTEM

An important element in altering the function of the state has been to establish a legal framework. "Stability in the long run cannot be achieved by the rule of man, but only by the rule of law . . . "[48] Law will allow a regularized, predictable method for handling much of the social conflict. Written law also creates a more democratic environment. Without law, people are mere supplicants, asking favors from officials with unrestricted power. With law, officials have limits set by law, and citizens can demand their rights.

Since 1978, China has been developing and strengthening its legal system. Organizational charters, criminal laws, marriage laws, environmental protection laws, laws dealing with foreign investment, and many other subjects have been drafted. Civil law is being regularized, and casebooks are being developed to clarify precedent in this area.[49] The sensitive matter of administrative law is still in the preparatory stage.[50] It is administrative law, however, that can provide a mechanism to oversee governmental actions and that can help create a legal environment for government action, with regularized procedures for controlling improper, arbitrary, and illegal actions by governmental officials. Some Chinese political scientists understand that procedures are crucial in shaping the types of outcomes that emerge from a political system.

China has been devoting substantial resources to training lawyers and judges, and explaining to local officials the need to obey, respect, and utilize law. By the end of 1986, China had seven law colleges and 33 law departments, turning out 4,000 graduates a year. A China National Lawyers' Association was established and a standardized examination was developed to certify lawyers. Roughly 40,000 enterprises had legal consultative offices.[51] There is a five-year plan to publicize laws at all levels of the government.[52]

Cases in which the government violates law were beginning to get into the courts. A public works department was held responsible by a court when a bicyclist suffered injuries at an unmarked trench in the road. In another case, a court agreed that Shanghai's environmental protection department could impose fines, despite party disagreement.[53]

However, China has many departments, which have issued countless regulations. The legal status of each one will take a long time to be sorted out. Moreover, for millenia China has had government of men, not of law. At best, acceptance of legal principles will be a gradual process, requiring years and decades.

Another problem is that the Chinese government reserves the right to annul laws.[54] Of course there is value in removing old, irrelevant laws whose enforcement makes no sense. But if laws can easily be annulled, then are they really laws?

The Chinese press reported some of the practical problems in strengthening the legal system. According to one report, defense lawyers were not being taken seriously. Working and living conditions were very bad, and funds were not available for legal research and case investigation. Sometimes lawyers discovered that the court verdict had been written before the trial. Under such conditions, some lawyers quit.[55] The fundamental principle of independence of the judiciary was a difficult problem in the environment of Communist Party leadership. The concept of innocence until proven guilty flies in the face of traditional acceptance of authority. The establishment of a comprehensive legal system will be very difficult, and slow at best.

One important dimension of law and due process involves handling criticisms of government workers. In the last decades, Chinese administration has been sabotaged by the politics of slander. Every day, letters pour into Chinese governmental organizations and newspapers. These letters criticize or expose bad policy, illegalities, and corruption. About 20–30 percent of these letters are anonymous. Such letters have provided crucial leads for criminal investigations.

Some charges are false and irresponsible. One survey found that 30 percent of the anonymous charges were false.[56] In the past, these charges were often accepted and entered onto peoples' secret, personal files maintained by the party branch of each unit. The victim was unaware of the charges and had no procedural safeguards to contest them. People were penalized without investigation and without any other basis. Later, agencies became totally absorbed in reevaluating the charges and decisions. (One theme in traditional Chinese politics and literature has been the importance of clearing the names of people who were "falsely accused."[57])

Such a pattern of work caused numerous problems. Petty jealousies were allowed to get out of hand. Administration was disrupted as people were attacked, sent to the countryside, jail or worse, and institutions were thrown into conflict. In this manner China was substantially paralyzed during the decade of 1966–1976.

Political writers in 1986 recognized the need to establish procedural safeguards to prevent a repeat of such "McCarthyism." Anonymous charges were to be investigated carefully to verify their accuracy, before being acted upon.

## REFORMS OF THE POLITICAL STRUCTURE

Although political reform became a crucial issue in 1986, it was not a completely new topic. Since the late 1970's, China's leaders had discussed political reforms and made some marginal changes. Still, by 1986, no structural changes had been made. Just as reforms to the industrial sector encountered complex problems in implementation, so too the implementation of political reforms was sharply limited.

Chinese political writers in 1986 offered no indication that substantive changes had been made in the political system. Yan Jiaqi, Director of the Institute of Political Science of the Chinese Academy of Social Sciences, outlined some of the problems:

... Highly concentrated power is the basic characteristic of our present political system. It is shown mainly in the following three respects:

1. We have never defined the scope of functions, powers, and responsibilities of the party organizations, as distinct from government organizations.... [P]arty organizations at all levels have, in practice, taken on business which should have been handled by organs of state power, namely the executive branch and the legislative branch ... [N]ot only does the party always function in place of the executive agencies, but also the system of the National People's Congress can not function effectively....

2. ... Powers are overcentralized, so that the initiative of local authorities can hardly be brought into full play. Even in the leading bodies of our party and government as well as in all kinds of enterprises and institutions, people's initiative can't be brought into full play....

3. We have never defined the scope of functions, powers, and responsibilities of the government organizations as distinct from those of economic enterprises and social institutions. The enterprises and institutions practically became subsidiary bodies of the executive organizations ... [58]

Chinese writers discussed division of power and responsibilities (*fen quan*) and checks and balances (*zhi heng*) to control government leaders. Western political forms were useful models, according to one writer:

Lenin once pointed out, "Socialism cannot win its victory unless it carries out full democracy." To carry on a full democracy, we cannot simply completely deny bourgeois democracy, which is still effective in today's world. We should actively absorb its rational parts. For example, the principle of "the separation of three powers" is an important element in capitalist republics. It has been proven by history to be an important measure in preventing the restoration of feudal dictatorships.... Undoubtedly the system of separation of power is a method to balance the capitalist forces and safeguard bourgeois rule. But there are some rational factors to check power organs, and to prevent administrative power from expanding viciously. It can be used as a theoretical reference point as we perfect mechanisms for restricting political power in the socialist state. [59]

Some of these principles have been applied to the locus of political power, the Chinese Communist Party. [60] In 1979–80, a Discipline Inspection Commission was set up to review party members' style and to root out corruption. A Central Secretariat was reestablished to provide better staff work. Party schools were revived, and recruitment efforts among intellectuals were expanded.

At the 12th Party Congress in 1982, slogans about democratization found their way into party documents and a new party constitution was adopted. To weaken the centralized structure and prevent a new one-man dictatorship, power was divided to three major units. The Central Committee had primary responsibility for making policy. The Discipline Inspection Commission was strengthened. It set up a parallel organization at every level to review party members. The Central Advisory Committee was composed of the most elderly leaders, who could continue to give broad advice without being involved in the details of policy formulation. The office of party chairman was converted to that of general secretary, a title implying more coordination rather than leadership. The general secretary "convened" the Political Bureau but "presided over" the Secretariat.

The purpose of these changes was to strengthen the capabilities and legitimacy of the party. Members of the party were to have better opportunities for participation. At the same time, reliance on the internal Discipline Inspection Commission to root out cases of abuse of power meant that mass participation in the party would play no particular role. These changes may have improved the effectiveness of the Communist Party, but they did not bring about a major reform of the political system.

Changes were also proposed for the National People's Congress. In theory, the National People's Congress is "the highest organ of state power." It is elected (indirectly) for a five year term. The current, 6th NPC has nearly 3,000 deputies. Its membership includes 13.5 percent minority nationality deputies, 21.2 percent women, and 37.5 percent nonCommunist Party personages. Its Standing Committee, with a chairman, 20 vice chairmen, and 133 members, meets roughly every two months. People's Congresses are elected at four levels: national, provincial, county, and township.[61]

After 1979, some efforts were made to give the National People's Congress a stronger role. A new election law in 1979 promised more direct elections at the county level, and proposed that there be more candidates than positions to be filled.[62] In the early 1980's, the National People's Congress did investigate and expose some cases of government incompetence and corruption.

Nevertheless, the discussions about political reform in 1986 did not suggest that the National People's Congress had become an effective, independent locus of political power. Many suggestions were made to expand the real power and improve the functioning of these congresses. One Chinese writer offered suggestions for these issues:

The People's Congress should . . . continuously improve its own quality of work, strengthen its organizational structure, and improve its capability and functions . . . The essence of the representative system is to require those people's delegates to represent the electorates' real will, to speak for the people, and to be responsible for their constituents.[63]

Another writer has offered more concrete suggestions:

The people's congresses and their standing committees at different levels have the power to make decisions on important affairs of their respective administrative areas... If the people's representative congress studies a proposal from the party, but does not adopt it, this is normal... [W]ith regard to the power to appoint and remove officials, the people's congresses at different levels have the power to elect and remove leaders of government and to approve government nominations of personnel in their respective administrative areas... In recent years, the people's congresses and their standing committees have carried out some supervisory work by hearing and examining governmental work reports, inspecting, addressing inquiries to the organs of the state, and so on. This has had some effect... Demanding explanations is one type of supervision. In recent years, this method of demanding explanation has been used too infrequently by the People's Representative Congress. It is used even less often by the Standing Committee.... In order to guarantee the quality of the deputies, we must use effectively democratic elections, training of deputies, and mass supervision. Elections must really embody a democratic spirit.[64]

Another writer commented:

[I]t is imperative to have explicit stipulations and safeguards regarding the quality of deputies, the process of producing deputies, the deputies' accountability to their constituencies, the deputies' actual undertaking of and their participation in all types of policy making work, and the concrete exercise of deputies' functions and powers (including the right of deliberation, the right to address inquiries, the right of impeachment, and the right of recall), so as to enable people's congresses to become highly authoritative organs that represent the extensive popular will and can effect very substantial results.[65]

To symbolize the new roles of the people's congresses, Yan Jiaqi suggested changing the name to "people's assemblies."[66]

In December 1986, China's election law was amended to make the people's congresses more democratic.[67] Previously, only grassroots congresses were elected directly, and higher levels were elected indirectly. The 1986 change expanded direct elections to the county level. (The 1979 law also had this provision. Apparently, it was amended away in the early 1980's.) The law has new qualifications for deputies to ensure they are more skilled socially and politically, and are not made deputies simply as an honor. More candidates must be nominated than the number of seats, so there are some real contests.[68]

The election law specifies that in provincial people's congresses, each deputy from rural areas will represent five times as many people as a city delegate. In the National People's Congress, rural delegates represent eight times as many people as city deputies.[69] These provisions ensure that urban delegates will be a majority in the congresses, despite the fact that China is 80 percent rural. Minority groups are also allowed some over-representation.[70]

Reforms were also made in state administration. Rural administration was changed. The rural people's communes were dissolved after 1982, and local government offices set up. The underlying principle was to separate economic enterprises from regular government administration. In addition, special districts, which had previously supervised rural counties, were eliminated, and rural counties were placed under the supervision of urban centers, to expand urban–rural exchanges.

These structural changes are related to an important shift in thinking. Chinese social scientists are recognizing that different people and groups in society have different economic interests.[71] Of course Mao Zedong had spoken of "nonantagonistic contradictions," but in general the communist party had argued that only one policy and viewpoint was correct. The Communist Party would select correct policy with little interference, and the state would implement it vigorously.

In thinking about representative organizations, Chinese political scientists now showed cautious interest in pluralism and interest groups. Su Shaozhi, director of the Research Institute of Marxism, Leninism, and Mao Zedong Thought, argued,

First, we must replace monism by pluralism when discussing interests . . . [Stalin's] monistic viewpoint is incomplete . . . Only when we acknowledge the differences and pluralism of interests can we make the correct decision . . . We should allow within the party free discussions among people holding different viewpoints. We must not simply take the words of leadership as the only thing that counts.[72]

Another writer acknowledged, "The pluralistic concept of interests is an issue worth studying."[73]

Acceptance of the idea of pluralism is significant because this is the first step in legitimating more political competition. Some interest groups are already being established, such as one for handicapped people and another for entrepreneurs.

In some cases, the representative organizations assumed more of an ombudsman role than a legislative role. In one fascinating case, a school in Hunan dismissed over 200 students to improve the academic rating of the school. Parents complained to the county People's Congress, which investigated and declared the dismissals to be a violation of law. (The article said nothing about the role of courts in this judicial determination.[74])

Some writers, such as the distinguished sociologist Fei Xiaotong, urged using the Chinese People's Political Consultative Conference to offer popular supervision. He argued this organization, which included many non-party personages and on which he served as vice chairman, could function like Great Britain's House of Lords.[75]

Another change was to expand the role of minor parties. China has eight residual parties left over from 1949. These include the Revolutionary Committee of the Nationalist Party, the Chinese Association for

Promoting Democracy, the China Democratic National Construction Association, the China Democratic League, the Chinese Peasants and Workers Democratic Party, the China Zhi Gong Party, the September 3 (*Jiu San*) Society, and the Taiwan Democratic Self-Government League. These parties had been suppressed and had dwindled as they got older. In recent years, they have been allowed to recruit new members, and have reached a total of about 160,000.[76] Of course this is a small number, about 3 percent of the membership of the Communist Party. The minor parties accept the principle of leadership of the Communist Party, and did not nominate candidates for election competition. They got budgetary support from the Communist Party and had no alternative funding.

Their main activity was to join in political discussion informally and in the Chinese People's Consultative Conference about policy and administration. The Chairman of the Chinese Peasants and Workers Democratic Party, 88-year-old Professor Zhou Gucheng from Fudan University's history department, is now a vice chairman of the Standing Committee of China's National People's Congress.[77] Fei Xiaotong became vice chairman of the China Democratic League in January 1987, and has been a vice chairman of the Chinese People's Consultative Conference since 1983.[78] Another vice chairman is noted physicist Qian Weichang. Lu Jiaxi, a leader of the Chinese Peasants and Workers Democratic Party, was the president of the Chinese Academy of Sciences until his dismissal in January 1987. Members of the Zhi Gong Party, active among returned overseas intellectuals particularly in Guangdong and Fujian provinces, have been elected to people's congresses at various levels.[79]

A member of the Politbureau of the Communist Party described the relationship between the Communist Party and other parties this way:

Leaders within the Communist Party should subject themselves to the supervision of the non-communists. They should study carefully their criticisms and suggestions, adopt the correct ones while giving honest answers to others.[80]

While the role of the democratic parties was to be expanded, real competition between parties was not to be allowed. Commentators still held that the Communist Party's "right of leadership is the outcome of the historical development of the past century and the premise for any plan of political restructuring."[81] The official minor parties accepted this arrangement. When demonstrations broke out in December 1986, the minor democratic parties did not support them. Instead, they supported the Communist Party's calls for social stability and gradual reform, at least in public.[82]

A few intellectuals, such as popular Shanghai writer Wang Ruowang, did discuss the idea of multi-party politics, but this was premature. The leadership of the Communist Party was the most important of the four cardinal principles. Wang was one of the victims of the attack on bourgeois liberalization in January 1987.[83]

Alternative methods for obtaining citizen input were tried in Guangzhou. The mayor's office set up a "hotline" for handling popular input and complaints. It received about 20 calls a day, many dealing with problems such as power shortages, noise, water and air pollution, other problems in public infrastructure, and complaints about practices in farmers' markets.[84] This could provide government with additional inputs without forcing a real sharing of political power.

Tianjin experimented with a different method to get citizen input. Since 1983 it has distributed questionnaires at the end of the year to 1,000 local families selected at random, to seek opinions on performance and their demands. Citizens asked for better cooking gas supplies and for a more open food marketing system. (It is not known to what extent the questionnaire restricted the options available to the respondents.)[85]

China also explored other mechanisms to monitor and control its bureaucrats. The Communist Party strengthened its inspection departments. The financial auditing systems and statistical offices were improved.[86] A new judicial arrangement was under development, with administrative courts under the supervision of the regular legal system. Interest was expressed in the Scandinavian ombudsman system.

A final and most sensitive issue in China's political system involved the status of Deng Xiaoping, aged 82. Would he gracefully retire and thereby strengthen the precedent for limited terms of office, and simultaneously begin to institutionalize regular turnover in leadership? Or would he stay in office until death, in the tradition of previous communist leaders and Chinese emperors? This issue was not discussed openly very much, but a few articles in fall 1986 advocated both that he retire and not retire. The liberal paper *Shenzhen Youth* urged Deng to step down, to set a good example in ending the life-tenure system. The paper was investigated by Beijing for this public suggestion.[87]

One Hong Kong analyst surmised that conservatives and particularly military forces wanted Deng to stay in office. They feared his formal retirement would give successor Hu Yaobang a protected environment in which to consolidate his power. Top military people, it was guessed, opposed Hu Yaobang, and his liberal cosmopolitan policies.[88] They wanted Hu out before Deng stepped down. Some analysts believe this debate on Deng's retirement was the spark that led to Hu Yaobang's forced retirement.

China is at an early stage in thinking and experimenting with political reform, but the process has started. The key point is that China has made substantial progress in bringing in a new generation of leaders.

The Thirteenth National Congress of the communist party in October 1987 is expected to go a long way toward clarifying the nature and timetable of political reform in China that these leaders want.[89]

## CIVIL LIBERTIES

In Western political thought, the foundation of democracy is in civil liberties. The Chinese Constitution, at Articles 35 and 36, recognizes freedom of speech, press, assembly, association, parade, demonstration, and religion. In practice, actual implementation of policy has not always respected these rights. China's political scientists realize, of course, that the important issue is not a few phrases in the constitution, but rather the manner in which these phrases are carried out. Su Shaozhi, the Director of the Institute of Study of Marxism, Leninism, and Mao Zedong Thought, has admitted, "law was frequently disobeyed, and what is more, the constitution was ignored. If you criticize someone for violating the constitution, many people will laugh at your foolishness. This is due to a cultural tradition of not having political democracy."[90]

In practice, there were important advances. Discussion was quite open at party and government meetings in 1986. People who made critical comments at meetings faced some risk, but efforts were made to protect them. The problems and progress were both suggested by a report from Hunan. In one county people's congress, one local representative accused the local party officials of incompetence and corruption. "They only seek to improve their own living standards," he charged, while farmers were suffering from a serious shortage of fuel that prevented them from operating flour mills, pumps, and tractors. The county party officials counterattacked, accusing their critic of having "anti-party opinions." The higher level party committee intervened, criticized the county party secretary for suppressing democracy, forced him to apologize in person, and used this incident to educate party members and officials in democracy and legal knowledge.[91]

Freedom of press was considered an important element in the political reforms. One Chinese writer observed that freedom of speech and publication was the basic condition for political democracy, which he said was the ultimate goal of China's political reforms.[92] In general the mass media were tightly controlled, but vigorous investigative reporting in recent years has exposed widespread corruption and incompetence. One of the main reporters has been Liu Binyan, who developed a large following. Some newspapers and magazines, generally with a limited readership, have been able to present a wide range of views.

A seminar in Harbin in August 1986, sponsored by the party's propaganda department, encouraged the members of the press to "free their minds, and dare to innovate." They should not have self-imposed restrictions, but instead should become the readers' "bosom friends."[93] China was reported to be discussing giving the press more autonomy from the party and drafting new laws about the press.[94]

*China Legal News* described some of the constraints on the press. When the press carried out effective investigative reporting and exposed incompetence or scandal, the criticized unit attempted to counterattack the press. It went to higher officials, charged the paper with libel, and refused future interviews. Precisely for such reasons, institutionalizing the independence of the press was necessary:

A free press can ensure people the right to criticize individuals or the government and voice their ideas.

Freedom of speech and publication is the basic condition for political democracy, which is the ultimate goal of China's political reform. To ensure this freedom, media and publication laws should be published.

So long as it does not violate the law, any speech or article should have the right to be published without interference from any quarter. Editors or editorial boards should have the right to decide what to publish. Intervention by any organization or individual should be taken as infringing upon civil rights.

The key to the reform of the press is that each newspaper should have adequate decision-making power. The party and the government should keep interference to a minimum.[95]

The book publishing industry has also seen big steps forward in recent years. In the mid 1980s it published a very broad range of books, including translations of many classical and contemporary Western works.

Chinese reformers were even thinking about the concept of privacy. One article urged that China develop a right to privacy with respect to private affairs, personal economics, family life, feelings, and religion. This would represent a fundamental change in Chinese culture and behavior.[96] In the system now in effect, a person's pre-marital or extra-marital relations are treated as social and political matters. They are noted in personal files and affect job assignments.

## EXPERIMENTS IN REFORM

By late 1986, a broad range of reforms had been proposed, but there is a long distance between proposal and policy. Some of the proposals were from intellectual visionaries, with little hope of adoption. Some were by serious, well-connected academics. Some were by government administrators who could actually try out their own ideas.

How would China begin to move from ideas for reform to an actual reform program? The Communist Party of China has always had a distinctive style of policy development and leadership. Social experiments play a major role. After theoretical discussions, social experiments are organized to test policy and to establish a demonstration that can be used for popularization. This pattern was followed in agriculture. Discussions in 1978/79 foreshadowed experiments for restructuring rural organization.[97] Likewise, institutional reforms in the industrial sector followed formal experiments in industry in certain localities.[98] Experiments in political reform in a few localities will point the path to future national reforms in politics.

In 1986 the Chinese leadership selected sixteen cities for experiments in structural reform. These are medium-sized cities in all regions of China.[99] One was Changzhou, a medium-sized industrial city located between Nanjing and Shanghai.[100] The central government carried out experiments in Changzhou to increase the responsiveness of enterprises to market signals. The autonomy of enterprise managers was increased. This required giving the enterprise manager full power and responsibility for managing the factory. The party organization in the enterprise was separated formally from the day-to-day management.

Another experimental city is Huangshi City in Hubei, where there were experiments with new forms of executive bodies, the separation of party and government functions, and the cadre system.

More overtly political experiments were carried out since 1985 in the Shekou industrial district in Shenzhen. This city, adjacent to the Hong Kong border, is a special economic area with more market-oriented policies. Crucial aspects of the experiment included: 1) popular election of all officials; 2) terms of office having limits rather than life-long terms; 3) the opportunity for voters to recall, or cast no-confidence votes for, managerial boards, and the obligation of these boards to resign after such a no-confidence vote; and 4) encouragement of public criticism and academic discussions of politics.[101] While this experiment is considered interesting by Chinese analysts, the conditions in Shekou are considered too atypical for the experiment to have broader implications. Shekou is very unusual in that it is a new town, inhabited by immigrants from all over China and having very open leadership style.

This phase of social experiments can easily last for three to five years. Not until then, at the earliest, is it possible to have broader experiments. Reforms in agriculture and industry have followed such a schedule, and the reform process in the political system will certainly take longer.

It should be noted that in the Soviet Union experiments in economic reform have been carried out periodically in a few test locations, but this usually has not led to major economic reform.[102]

The precise significance of the political reforms that have been implemented is hard to gauge. By 1986 there were only marginal changes to the existing structure. The reforms did not fundamentally redistribute political or economic power, or fundamentally change the legitimacy of the political system, but they could begin to reduce the inefficiencies, blunders, and corruption that could further undermine legitimacy. Moreover, these kinds of reforms may create a political dynamic that could lead to more significant reforms over a period of a few decades. Plans were underway to test the reforms at several sites as the first step of a long-term systematic implementation process.

The Central Committee was very explicit that there was no readily available model for China in either economic or political reform. Adequate surveys and research regarding Chinese circumstances were the only means to determine the aims, methods, and steps of reform. For this reason, the Central Committee decided that political reform was not scheduled for completion within four or five years, and should be carried out step by step. Chinese were urged to be aware of the urgency for reform, and also to be patient.[103] *People's Daily* editorialized, "A long process is needed to build up a socialist political structure that is highly democratic, efficient, and with a complete legal system. This cannot be realized overnight."[104] Song Tingming, a deputy bureau director of the State Commission for Economic Structural Reform, estimated that ten years would be needed for reform of the economic and political structures.[105]

As for the views of the Chinese people, one survey indicated that 50 percent of the people thought that the reform was moving slowly or too slowly; only 21 percent thought reforms were proceeding at a proper rate.[106] My students supported reform, but feared it might take a long time, perhaps centuries.

Deeply embedded in the discussion, proposals, and experiments about political reform was a crucial contradiction. Were the long-term goals of reform to change fundamentally the nature of the communist political system? Were they designed ultimately to replace the dictatorship of the proletariat, operating through the Communist Party, by a democratically elected multi-party system? Some reformers had this goal. Alternatively, were the reforms designed to improve the efficiency and legitimacy of communist party rule so it could continue indefinitely? Deng Xiaoping had this objective.

To the extent that programs could simultaneously help both long-term policies, there would be agreement on them. Strengthening the legal system, bringing in younger cadres, narrowing and clarifying the responsibilities of the party, expanding opportunities for discussion and political input; these are some examples. But to the extent that proposals forced a choice in the long-term goals, there were problems. The issues of real decision-making power and retirement of senior leaders to make way for a new generation seemed to some to be such difficult choices. These problems ultimately exploded in December and January of 1986/87.

## NOTES

1. Zhi Mu, "Strengthening the people's congress is the fundamental way to develop socialist democracy," *World Economic Herald* (Aug. 2, 1986). Available in Benedict Stavis (ed.), "Reform of China's political system," *Chinese Law and Government*, 20:1 (Spring 1987).

2. "Step by step," *China Daily* (Jan. 26, 1987), p. 4.

3. Zhou Mianwei, "The right to use the slogans of democracy, liberty, and human rights does not belong only to the bourgeoisie," *Daily Worker* (Aug. 11, 1986), p. 4; FBIS (Aug. 19, 1986), p. K 5.

4. Andrew Nathan, *Chinese Democracy* (New York: Knopf, 1985).

5. Elizabeth Perry and Christine Wong, *The Political Economy of Reform in Post-Mao China* (Cambridge: Harvard Council on East Asian Studies, 1985).

6. "Shenzhen lures skilled," *China Daily* (Dec. 23, 1986), p. 3.

7. This was the view of factory managers I interviewed in Changzhou, Oct. 31–Nov. 1, 1986. Exactly the same observation was made by the mayor of Shenyang, Wu Disheng, "Shenyang takes the lead in urban reform," *China Daily* (Dec. 11, 1986), p. 4.

8. "Looking at other's reforms," *China Daily* (Nov. 26, 1986), p. 4; *Economic Development and Systematic Reform*, no. 1 (1987).

9. Gao Ling, "Why the draft enterprise bankruptcy law has not been adopted—sidelight of the NPC standing committee session," *Liaowang Overseas Edition*, no. 39 (Sept. 29, 1986), pp. 13–14; FBIS (Oct. 7, 1986), p. K 1.

10. "NPC again mulls revised draft of bankruptcy law," *China Daily*, (Nov. 17, 1986), p. 1.

11. "China adopts trial enterprise bankruptcy law," *China Daily* (Dec. 3, 1986), p. 1. The text is available at FBIS (Dec. 5, 1986), p. K 1.

12. "Workers desire flexibility in jobs," *China Daily* (Jan. 5, 1987), p. 3.

13. "Old-style banking hinders economy," *China Daily* (Dec. 13, 1986), p. 4.

14. "China to levy tax on higher earners," *China Daily* (Dec. 13, 1986), p. 3.

15. Li Yiming, "A conception of reform of the ownership system in our country," *People's Daily* (Sept. 26, 1986), p. 5; FBIS (Oct. 22, 1986), p. K 5.

16. "Leasing business proves invigorating," *China Daily* (Dec. 9, 1986), p. 4. Based on Wang Shaofei, "On a new pattern of socialist ownership," *Guangming Ribao* (Nov. 1986).

17. "Auction for shops in Beijing," *China Daily* (Dec. 1, 1986), p. 3.

18. "Auction of shop a first for Shanghai," *China Daily* (Dec. 9, 1986), p. 2; "Shenyang takes lead in urban reform," *China Daily* (Dec. 11, 1986), p. 4.

19. "Financial market to make debut in Beijing," *China Daily* (Dec. 24, 1986), p. 1.

20. Zhang Duo, "A brief discussion on the orientation of reform of state-owned enterprises," *Bright Daily* (Dec. 6, 1986); FBIS (Dec. 18, 1986), p. K 19.

21. "More private health care encouraged," *China Daily* (Jan. 8, 1987), p. 3; "Taxi firm in high gear," *China Daily* (Dec. 29, 1986), p. 6.

22. "Private traders seek protection," *China Daily* (Jan. 8, 1987), p. 4.

23. "Private businesses need special rules," *China Daily* (Dec. 29, 1986), p. 4.

24. "Problems of being an entrepreneur," *China Daily* (Dec. 20, 1986), p. 4.

25. Wang Shuwei, "A summary of the discussions on the labor force market," *Bright Daily* (Aug. 2, 1986), p. 3; FBIS (Aug. 14, 1986), p. K 16.

26. "Iacocca," *China Daily* (Dec. 20, 1986), p. 4.

27. Chen Wenxi, "Freedom of job choice essential," *China Daily* (Nov. 6, 1986), p. 4.

28. "Workers desire flexibility in jobs."

29. Wang Ningjun, "Majority of graduates assigned by state," *China Daily* (July 23, 1986), p. 1.

30. Jerome Alan Cohen and Ta-kuang Chang, "New foreign investment provisions," *Chinese Business Review* (Jan./Feb. 1987), pp. 11–15.

31. "A blueprint is needed for reform of the political structure," *Beijing Review*, no. 20 (May 18, 1987), p. 16.

32. "It is necessary to study how to further reform the political structure," *Red Flag*, no. 15 (Aug. 1, 1986), p. 2; FBIS (Aug. 13, 1986), p. K 3.

33. Lo Ping, "Note on a northern journey—A Yao Wenyuan type hatchet man has gone on the stage—dispute on the political reform between those in power and the public," *Zheng Ming*, no. 110 (Dec. 1, 1986), pp. 9–12; FBIS (Dec. 12, 1986), p. K 13.

34. "Party role new—but vital," *China Daily* (Dec. 11, 1986), p. 4.

35. "New rules promote factory director management role," *China Daily* (Jan. 12, 1987).

36. Zhang Youyu, "Reform of the political system and the division of the work of party and government," *Bright Daily* (Oct. 29, 1986). Available in Benedict Stavis (ed.), "Reform of China's political system," *Chinese Law and Government*, 20:1 (Spring 1987).

37. Zhi Mu, "Strengthening the people's congress is the fundamental way to develop socialist democracy," *World Economic Herald* (Aug. 11, 1986). Available in Benedict Stavis (ed.), "Reform of China's political system," *Chinese Law and Government*, 20:1 (Spring 1987).

38. Lo Ping, "Note on a Northern journey—A Yao Wenyuan type hatchet man...."

39. Michel Oksenberg, "The exit pattern from Chinese politics and its implications," *China Quarterly*, no. 67 (Sept. 1976), pp. 501–518.

40. Christopher M. Clarke, "Rejuvenation, reorganization and the dilemmas of modernization in post-Deng China," *Journal of International Affairs*, 39:2 (Winter, 1986), pp. 119–132; David S. G. Goodman, "The National CCP Conference of Sept. 1985 and China's leadership change," *China Quarterly* no. 105 (March 1986), pp. 123–130.

41. The following material is based largely on discussions I had with the Shanghai Old Cadre Bureau, November 28, 1986. See also Yan Mei-ning, "Further comments on Hu," *Hong Kong Standard* (Feb. 8, 1987), p. 9; FBIS (Feb. 9, 1987), p. K 5.

42. "Reforms change cadre system," *China Daily* (April 3, 1987).

43. "Unqualified cadres to be demoted, party says," *China Daily* (Jan. 6, 1987), p. 1.

44. "Party in Shaanxi assails corruption," *China Daily* (Oct. 21, 1986), p. 3.

45. "New rules zero in on nepotism," *Beijing Review*, no. 8 (Feb. 24, 1986), pp. 4–6.

46. Lo Ping, "Sudden rise of calls for Qiao Shi to become General Secretary," *Zheng Ming*, no. 108 (Oct. 1, 1986), pp. 6–8; FBIS (Oct. 10, 1986), pp. K 1–2.

47. "Public assessment of officials urged," *China Daily* (Dec. 11, 1986), p. 4.

48. Li Kejing, "China's political restructuring . . . ," p. 15.

49. William Jones (ed.), "Civil law in China," *Chinese Law and Government*, 18:3–4 (Fall/Winter, 1985/86).

50. Lecture by Prof. Gong Xiangrui at Fudan University, December 1, 1986.

51. "Enterprises set up legal consulting offices," *NCNA* (Oct. 7, 1986); FBIS (Oct. 10, 1986), p. K 9. Wang Gangyi, "Reform revives role of lawyers," *China Daily* (March 18, 1987).

52. "Law drive 'vital'—Qiao," *China Daily* (Dec. 23, 1986), p. 3.

53. Zhang Sutang, "People's Courts file lawsuits against government," *NCNA* (Nov. 14, 1986); FBIS (Nov. 20, 1986), p. K 10.

54. "Old laws annulled in consolidation," *China Daily* (Jan. 12, 1987), p. 3.

55. "Too few lawyers—even more quitting," *China Daily* (Nov. 29, 1986), p. 3.

56. "Anonymous critics reflect truth," *China Daily* (Nov. 18, 1986), p. 4.

57. In the year 1303, 5,176 wrongs were redressed. This quest for justice is a common theme in Chinese traditional opera. Lu Zhidong, "13th Century Drama, 'Snow in Midsummer,' " *China Reconstructs* (Sept. 1986), p. 43.

58. Yan Jiaqi, "Our current political system and the goals of reform," *Liberation Daily* (Aug. 13, 1986). Available in Benedict Stavis (ed.), "Reform of China's political system," *Chinese Law and Government*, 20:1 (Spring 1987).

59. Wei Haibo, "Reform of the Political System and Political Democratization," *Legal Studies*, no. 10 (1986). Available in Benedict Stavis (ed.), "Reform of China's political system," *Chinese Law and Government*, 20:1 (Spring 1987).

60. Tony Saich, "Party building since Mao-A question of style?" in Neville Maxwell and Bruce McFarlane, *China's Changed Road to Development* (Oxford: Pergamon Press, 1984), pp. 149–167; Lowell Dittmer, "The 12th Congress of the Communist Party of China," *China Quarterly* no. 93 (March 1983), pp. 108–124; Graham Young, "Control and style: Discipline Inspection Commission since the 11th Congress," *China Quarterly* no. 97 (March 1984); Li Kejin, "China's political restructuring . . . ," p. 23.

61. Yang Xiaobing, "NPC: Its position and role," *Beijing Review*, no. 13 (March 30, 1987), pp. 17–21.

62. Brantly Womack, ed., "Electoral Reform in China," *Chinese Law and Government* 15:3–4 (Fall-Winter 1982–83).

63. Zhi Mu, "Strengthening the people's congress is the fundamental way to develop socialist democracy," *World Economic Herald* (Aug. 11, 1986). Available in Benedict Stavis (ed.), "Reform of China's political system," *Chinese Law and Government*, 20:1 (Spring 1987).

64. Pu Xingzu, "Increase the authority of the legislative bodies," *Political Science Research*, no. 2 (1986), pp. 15–17. Available in Benedict Stavis (ed.), "Reform of China's political system," *Chinese Law and Government*, 20:1 (Spring 1987).

65. Hu Ping, "Reflections on making policies democratically and scientifically," *People's Daily* (Dec. 8, 1986), p. 5; FBIS (Dec. 17, 1986), p. K 1.

66. "Yan Jiaqi proposes that 'People's Congresses' be changed to People's

Assemblies in the 1990's," *Zhongguo tongxun she* (Sept. 11, 1987); FBIS (Sept. 19, 1986), p. K 20.

67. The text of the amended election law is available in FBIS (Dec. 8, 1986), pp. K 2–10. See also "Wang Hanbin explains NPC electoral law revision," *NCNA* (Nov. 15, 1986); FBIS (Nov. 21, 1986), pp. K 6–8. Zhang Shangzhuo, "New developments in China's election system," *Bright Daily* (Jan. 25, 1987), p. 3; FBIS (Feb. 9, 1987), p. K 14.

68. Article 27. Yang Xiaobing, "NPC: Its position and role," *Beijing Review*, no. 13 (March 30, 1987), pp. 17–21.

69. Articles 12, 14.

70. Article 16.

71. "Interest groups must be heeded," *China Daily* (March 19, 1987), p. 4.

72. Kung Shuang-yin, "Director of the Research Institute of Marxism, Leninism, and Mao Zedong Thought under the Academy of Social Sciences of China on political reform," *Ta Kung Pao* (Sept. 17, 1986); FBIS (Sept. 29, 1986), p. K 16.

73. Li Kejing, "China's political restructuring . . . ," p. 23.

74. "Dismissal of poor students sparks row," *China Daily* (Oct. 20, 1986).

75. Xu Hong, "Power should be placed under the supervision of the people—Fei Xiaotong on political structural reform in China," *NCNA* (July 30, 1986); FBIS (July 31, 1986), p. K 2.

76. "Democratic parties work for modern China," *Beijing Review*, no. 8 (Feb. 24, 1986), pp. 19–21.

77. "Party leaders," *China Daily* (Jan. 5, 1987), p. 3.

78. "Fei Xiaotong discusses political structural reform," *CPPCC Journal* (July 8, 1986); FBIS (July 30, 1986), p. K 4; *NCNA* (July 30, 1986); FBIS (July 31, 1986), p. K 2. "Officers elected," *NCNA* (Jan. 9, 1987); FBIS (Jan. 15, 1987), p. K 37.

79. Li Zhongbo, "The China Zhi Gong Dang musters its forces again," *NCNA* (Oct. 3, 1986); FBIS (Oct. 7, 1986), p. K 12.

80. "Democratic parties 'have key role,' " *China Daily* (Dec. 5, 1986), p. 3.

81. Li Kejing, "China's political restructuring . . . ," p. 10.

82. Wu Naitao, "Intellectuals and bourgeois liberalization," *Beijing Review*, no. 15 (April 13, 1987), p. 21.

83. Zhang Zhenlu, "See the essence of bourgeois liberalization from Wang Ruowang's remarks," *People's Daily* (Jan. 18, 1987), p. 4; FBIS (Jan. 21, 1987), p. K 25.

84. "Thousands call city's hotline," *China Daily* (Jan. 9, 1987), p. 3.

85. "Polls help to improve Tianjin," *China Daily* (Jan. 8, 1987), p. 3.

86. "Audit chief bids to curb financial irregularity," *China Daily* (Dec. 8, 1986), p. 1.

87. Yau Shing-mu, "Youth paper 'pardoned' for Deng retirement items," *Hong Kong Standard* (Nov. 27, 1986), p. 8; FBIS (Nov. 28, 1986), p. K 12.

88. Lo Ping, "Disputes inside the party between the faction which wants Deng to stay and the faction which wants Deng to retire," *Zheng Ming*, no. 110 (Dec. 1, 1986), p. 6–8; FBIS (Dec. 4, 1986), p. K 9.

89. "Deng: Plan for political reform will come in fall," *China Daily* (March 20, 1987); *Beijing Review*, no. 13 (March 30, 1987).

90. Su Shaozhi, "The precondition for reform of political institutions is get-

ting rid of feudal pernicious influences," *People's Daily* (Aug. 15, 1986). Available in Benedict Stavis (ed.), "Reform of China's political system," *Chinese Law and Government*, 20:1 (Spring 1987).

91. "An incident of wantonly interfering in the work of the people's congress occurs in Shaoyang County, Hunan Province," *People's Daily* (Nov. 7, 1986), p. 1; FBIS (Nov. 12, 1986), p. K 1. "Reprimanded Official Admits Faults," *China Daily* (Nov. 17, 1986), p. 3.

92. Xiang Pu, "Media reform stirs lively public debate," *China Daily* (Sept. 29, 1986), p. 4.

93. Zhang Chijian, "Provincial newspaper editors hold forum under the auspices of CPC propaganda department," *People's Daily* (Aug. 19, 1986). "Teng Teng, deputy director of Propaganda Department of CPC Central Committee, speaks on press reform," *People's Daily* (Aug. 20, 1986); FBIS (Aug. 25, 1986), pp. K 4–5.

94. "Draft law on journalism to be ready 'next year,' " *South China Morning Post* (Sept. 2, 1986); FBIS (Sept. 5, 1986), p. K 9.

95. As reported in "Press Must Defend its Role as Critic," *China Daily* (Nov. 7, 1986), p. 4.

96. *Workers Daily*, cited by NCNA (Nov. 3, 1986); FBIS (Nov. 13, 1986), p. K 5.

97. David Shambaugh (ed.), "Zhao Ziyang's 'Sichuan Experience,' " *Chinese Law and Government*, 15:1 (Spring 1982), pp. 3–13.

98. Sidney Shapiro, *Experiment in Sichuan, a report on economic reform* (Peking: New World Press, 1981).

99. *People's Daily* (Aug. 29, 1986).

100. The following discussion of the Changzhou experiments is based on discussion with officials at Changzhou in October 31–November 1, 1986. See also "An 'Economic Star' Rises Through Performance," and "Changzhou Profits From Reforms," *Beijing Review*, no. 24 (June 16, 1986), pp. 14–20. Another test site is at Weifang in Shandong. "China to Extend Scope of Reform," *China Daily* (June 9, 1986), p. 4.

101. "Young Seek Better Democracy," *China Daily* (Nov. 10, 1986), p. 4.

102. Darrell Slider, Social experiments and Soviet policy making. Ph.D. Dissertation, Yale, 1981.

103. "Steady political reform urged," *China Daily* (Dec. 10, 1986), p. 4.

104. *Renmin Ribao* (Dec. 25, 1986), cited in "Anarchism is not democracy," *China Daily* (Dec. 26, 1986), p. 4.

105. Kung Shuangyun, "Government structural reform to take 10 years: problem of overstaffed organs hard to solve," *Ta Kung Pao* (Sept. 13, 1986), p. 3; FBIS (Sept. 16, 1986), p. K 1.

106. "Workers desire flexibility in jobs," *China Daily* (Jan. 5, 1987), p. 3.

# 3
# *Obstacles to Reform*

Despite all the interest in political reform, there was also much opposition, particularly against radical reforms that would change the basic system and personnel. At a broad level of abstraction, China's political culture has not supported democratic reforms. At a concrete level, political reforms were opposed by some important leaders for both ideological and personal reasons. Moreover, many groups received some benefits from the existing system, and each could veto (or at least slow down) efforts to change. The situation bears some similarity to the idea of gridlock in the analysis of stagflation in the United States.[1]

The forces opposed to reform had placed limits on reform at the Beidaihe meetings in summer 1986. This chapter will review the nature of the opposition. A later chapter will describe how they continued to resist reform at high level meetings and in publications during the fall and eventually used the student demonstrations to blunt the movement for radical structural reform, at least for a while.

## POLITICAL CULTURE

China's political culture has deep obstacles to democratic reform. Since the time of Confucius over two thousand years ago, Chinese people have assumed and almost hoped that government would be authoritarian. An authoritarian government was needed to prevent chaos. Lacking Aristotle's analytical perspective, Chinese political thought never focused on the issue of participation, and never conceptualized democracy as a political form that could or should exist.

Historically, China has been characterized by a cyclical pattern of order and chaos. Over decades or centuries, a strong government would become wealthy. This set the stage for corruption. Then the government became unable to maintain the rural economy. Flood, drought, and famine would become widespread. The government would raise taxes and military requisitions to try to maintain order. This increased both the suffering and the opportunities for corruption.

Finally, when people judged the government had lost its "mandate of heaven," there would follow widespread rebellion. Secret societies in the countryside often provided the leadership nucleus. Because the old society was ruled by Confucian intellectuals located in the major administrative cities, the tradition of rebellion was anti-intellectual and anti-urban. The rebellious spirit could be extremely cruel and violent, as people struggled desperately for survival and took revenge for previous suffering.

Some scholars have argued that the origin of the tension between order and chaos has psychological roots in group socialization practices (especially those of the family), which repress all manifestations of aggression. This brings feelings of insecurity and potentials for violence. "Thus, Chinese politics can at one moment be more orderly than most and at the next violent and hostile."[2]

Whether chaos is simply a historical pattern or has its own psychological roots, the period of chaos has always been dreaded. It was seen as a time of civil war, flood, drought, and famine. Suffering was enormous, with death and family disintegration. One example of chaos was the period of the three kingdoms during the third century, a period that looms large in Chinese consciousness because of its importance in Chinese literature. In such a period, moral behavior is virtually impossible. Survival required reliance on brute force and deceit.[3]

Finally a strongman would conquer China, establishing order and a new dynasty. Dictatorial government was not considered so terrible. It was far preferable to chaos. The "great" political leaders in Chinese history are those who brutally established national unity and order. When the government was strong enough to prevent chaos, the remaining issue was whether it would be enlightened authoritarianism or tyrannical authoritarianism. At a personal level, a strategy for self-preservation has traditionally been to form and utilize personal relationships based on reciprocity and to join factions of powerful people.[4]

A related aspect of China's political culture has been that since Confucius, the Chinese have considered the state to be an extension of familial authority (and vice versa). Indeed, the Chinese word for country (*guojia*) includes the character for family (*jia*).[5] The political ruler had as much right to rule his nation as a father had to rule his family. People have been expected to obey political leaders without question with the same discipline that they show when obeying their fathers. Rebellion against the state had the same moral connotation as rebellion against the father.[6] The political leader was leader for life, just as a father was a father for life. Written laws and the idea of elections were of no relevance, either for the family or for the state.[7]

Whether the state was viewed as a way to prevent chaos or as a large family, it was based on authoritarianism. One scholar summed up the core of traditional Chinese political culture, "Make decisions for the people. Do not let the people make their own decisions."[8]

The concept of democracy was antithetical to traditional Chinese political culture for several reasons. Philosophically, Chinese culture did not accept concepts of popular sovereignty or equality. Neither in the family nor in the political system could relationships of equality exist. Chinese culture did not share Western religion's idea of equality in the eyes of God.[9] The Chinese never thought that people should elect their own governors, any more than they could freely select their own parents.

China did not have political theorists comparable to Hobbes, Locke, or Rousseau, who suggested that the people themselves created government, and therefore the government should be responsible to the people. China never had an Adam Smith, who argued that autonomous market interactions of free people, without state interference, would lead to socially optimal results.

A seventeenth century Ming dynasty scholar-official, Huang Tsung-hsi, is known as China's Rousseau. Huang offered a scathing critique of official corruption and called for law and reform. Still, his proposals were within the age-old framework of the Confucian state.[10]

China did have a tradition of laws. In the Chinese legalist tradition, law strengthened the state and systematized the exercise of state power. This was different from Western ideas in which the legal system limited government power and provided a framework for free markets.

On a practical level, Chinese modalities of political input have always been extremely limited. Officials could politely make observations, if invited to do so by the emperor. China did have a tradition of liberalism that urged rulers and administrators to be honest and upright. A good official was urged to oppose bureaucracy and uncover corruption, even at risk to himself. The Ming Dynasty official Hai Rui was a famous example.[11] Chinese thought emphasized that the political leaders should follow ethical values and conform to rites and rituals. All this was within the Confucian framework and was designed to make the authoritarian state more humane and popular. It left decision-making power with the rulers, and did not convert the authoritarian state to Western-style democracy.

For Chinese there was no middle course between authoritarianism and chaos. There was no concept of institutionalized political participation through legal, regular channels. These were, of course, the core issues for all Western political thought since Aristotle. If they did not risk rebellion or lacked personal connections, Chinese could only yearn for upright officials.[12] Western-style democracy reminds Chinese more of chaos than of strong government. The competing parties, public arguments, and street demonstrations all resonate with chaos, not with strong, stable, unified government.

Given the weakness of structured social input into the political system and the weakness of the legal system, Chinese elite politics has often been largely a struggle between factions.[13] Ideological statements have often served as flags to identify the camps and their alignments.[14] Most Chinese leaders are "pragmatic," but Chinese pragmatism is based on a situational ethic and evaluation of practical needs. It can result in rapidly changing tactics. It is not based on commitment to fixed procedures.[15]

For at least a century, many Chinese have considered the traditional political culture to present problems. For the past century, they have wanted to modernize and to strengthen China so it could compete with the West. They noticed that some successful countries in the West had democratic political systems, with widespread popular participation, well-defined political institutions, and coherent legal frameworks. Some Chinese modernizers have argued that China needed such a system, too. In as much as Chinese political philosophy lacks the concept of democracy (in a Western way), the very concept of democracy is inherently Western. For China to democratize requires the Chinese to raise fundamental questions about the relationship between their own heritage and Western civilization.

China's reformers first changed the imperial system, at the turn of the century, and then overthrew it in 1911. After much struggle Sun Yat-sen emerged as China's main leader. His ideology included "Three People's Principles," roughly translated as nationalism, democracy, and people's welfare. Nevertheless, democracy could not be implemented immediately in China's traditional environment. The slogan of democracy was transformed to "tutelary democracy," implying people needed education and training in democracy. Western-style democracy was put off into the indefinite future. Whether under nationalist or communist leadership, establishing and maintaining democratic institutions have been insurmountable challenges so far in this century.

Contemporary political writers point out that traditional political values continue to be important. Some of the strongest comments were made by the Director of the Institute of Study of Marxism, Leninism, and Mao Zedong Thought, Su Shaozhi:

China is a country with a 2,000 year history of being a feudal society. This land was under a unified authoritarian empire for a long time. Although the autocratic monarchy no longer existed before liberation, the feudal influences haven't been weakened yet. After liberation, we didn't accomplish the task of mopping up the influence produced by the remaining feudalism in political ideology. Today, in the course of Chinese reform, how to clear up the surviving influences of feudalism still continues to be one of the most pressing problems. It is a prerequisite for carrying out the political structural reforms in the fields of politics, ideology, and culture.

First, the influence of feudalism in political ideology demonstrates itself in privileges. As it is, the public often talks about "unhealthy tendencies," which is the case when the cadres in the party and government and their children engage in business, and when officials are appointed in line with favoritism. These problems are all examples of special privileges, and privileges are deeply marked by feudalism. Such problems as engaging in trade and appointing people can never be considered a capitalist entrepreneurial spirit or a capitalist commodity relationship. They employ feudal remnants to undermine the national economy and to spoil the party's prestige. Privileges not only affect construction and development in our society; they also show up in culture as cultural autocracy. Before the "Great Cultural Revolution," and especially during that time, there existed cultural autocracy. After the Third Plenary Session of the 11th Central Committee and even nowadays, we can't say that remnants in this field have been wiped out completely ...

The pernicious influence of feudalism in political ideology will enable a lot of good, revolutionary practices to be "deformed." It can't bring about any good results; on the contrary, it brings difficulties and troubles.[16]

Traditional values remain because in many ways the contemporary Leninist-Stalinist communist system echoes and reinforces the traditional Confucian imperial pattern. The communist system has a highly structured bureaucracy whose legitimacy rests on "historical necessity." This source of legitimacy is much closer to "fate of heaven" or "divine right" than it is to "consent of the governed." One Chinese writer highlighted the similarity of the soviet pattern with China's traditional forms of rule:

We have not given adequate attention to analyzing the harm of copying the Soviet pattern in its entirety. The Soviet pattern ... closely combined with the remnants of feudalism, has produced a very bad effect with our thinking, our ideological state, and many of our concepts in the cultural field also ...[17]

It is ironic that the revolutionary system that set out to change the old system, and did in fact change it in many ways, also reinforced and strengthened some old patterns. Marx observed that any new society will bear the imprint of the old.

Despite Marxism's emphasis on class analysis and class loyalties, the close connection between family and politics remains. The strength of family values means that universal values are not accepted. Political appointments and business connections often follow family lines, with unfortunate consequences for broader interests.

The close connection between politics and ethics has caused other problems. It has led to desires to have officials both socialist minded and vocationally proficient. In practice, many officials have been neither. Moreover, positions in formal political organizations (such as the people's congresses) were awarded as honors to model workers, and not to people with independent political leadership capabilities. The political system was permeated by an atmosphere of gratitude. Lower officials felt obliged to higher officials for appointing them and were unwilling to criticize them.[18]

The highly disciplined environment of home, school, and state has undermined self-discipline and self-control, some contemporary Chinese scholars argue. As a result, weak government does not inspire voluntary self-help activities. Instead of constructive collective action, there is individual chaotic action. Sun Yat-sen referred to the Chinese people as being as disorganized as a pan of loose sand, precisely for this reason.

It is surprising that there has as yet been little discussion about education reforms to create a more democratic political culture. Chinese school children still sit erect, with hands folded behind their backs. They recite in unison, and stand when speaking. Political theorists throughout history have always stressed education to change values of the next generation. The degree to which China does this will be one indicator of their seriousness in democratic reform.

In the West, democratic governments did not emerge until centuries after feudalism started to decline. The ideas of limited governmental power, of popular sovereignty, of rule by law—these ideas all had roots in antiquity, but were not realized until the nineteenth and twentieth centuries, after a century or more of capitalist development. The bourgeoisie had created a culture of freedom and competition. Industrialization had brought new class structures and new patterns of economic growth, which led to new ways of resolving economic conflicts.

Is it possible for China's feudal political culture to change more rapidly, especially in the absence of a lengthy capitalist stage? An orthodox Marxist might be dubious. Some Chinese assume China will require centuries of gradual cultural transformation, just as the West has.

## OPPOSITION OF THE POLITICAL ELITES

Opposition to political reform came from some party and military elites. They had many reasons to fear and resist reforms. Some leaders feared economic problems would result from a free market orientation and a reduction in the state economic control systems. These changes

might bring higher, Western-induced consumption rates; lower investment rates in means of production for future growth; greater inflation,
inequality, and price and political instabilities; more internal migration;
and possible domestic conflict, which could have serious economic repercussions. Rapid social and economic change could also aggravate
ethnic cleavages and undermine confidence in existing culture. Social
relations could be weakened, so that people might be easily recruited by
opposition political groups. There were, in fact, indications that these
problems were emerging.

Conservatives could also point out that several Asian economies, such
as Taiwan, South Korea, Singapore, and Hong Kong have had rapid
growth rates while keeping authoritarian political systems. Authoritarian
politics might be needed to prevent the stresses of economic growth (or
stagnation) from becoming destabilizing. In contrast, they could point
to the political instability and tension in rapidly-modernizing Iran under
the Shah and in the reasonably democratic Punjab India and Sri Lanka,
or to the economic stagnation in many countries in Latin America, Asia,
and Africa.

The party and military elites argued on the positive side that China
already has a special, a better form of democracy, a proletarian democracy, that assures political power to China's working classes. Bourgeois
democracy is a sham, they said, and simply gives democracy to the
bourgeoisie. Senior conservative leader Peng Zhen spoke on November
25, 1986, to this effect.[19] China's system of economic planning needed
adjustment and improvement, not structural reform. Some Chinese
scholars urged, "to ensure that economic restructuring can achieve a
breakthrough and win a decisive victory, a systematic reform of political
structure should be put off until the 1990s."[20]

These theoretical analyses were reinforced by personal considerations.
Generally speaking, reforms would work to the disadvantage of many
leaders. Most obviously, the forced retirement of cadres 60 years old (or
perhaps 70 for top level cadres) meant a drastic change for them. Some
complained bitterly.[21]

For younger cadres, economic reforms would weaken their power. If
enterprises had more autonomy to respond to market forces, they would
be less responsive to political demands. Bureaucrats would lose much
autonomy in making their decisions, and would have less patronage.
They would no longer be able to offer jobs to relatives, friends, and
political allies. They would have fewer chances to squeeze enterprises
for funds. They would not be able to justify countless meetings at expensive guest houses at major scenic sights. Indeed, the reforms are
designed precisely to have these results.

Political reforms would, of course, directly undercut the stability and power of leaders. Even if there were no elections, a consultative process could be uncomfortable. A serious legislative inquiry could be unnerving. A vigorous investigative press could be disastrous.

Even reforms of the legal system could be problematic. Laws have the precise effect of reducing the arbitrary power of bureaucrats. In these ways, political reform hurts the short-term personal interests of some high-level cadres.

Thus many leaders endorsed the general principle of gradual reform (especially after they retired), but resisted any reform that might weaken their own personal positions. They were quite content with the old authoritarian system, which gave them much power and substantial security. Reform could only mean less power and more uncertainty, and this was enough reason to resist reform. A Hong Kong analyst observed, "The more power one has in his hands, the more reluctant he is to hand over or share his power." Both conservative and radical reformers had something in common in this regard.[22]

Deng Xiaoping himself pointed out that many bureaucrats were less than enthusiastic about implementing reforms that would reduce their own power and privileges:

There are a very few people who openly object to the reform. However, when it comes to matters concerning certain people's interests, some people who favor reform will also turn into a sort of obstacle. . . . We should be prudent and guard against rashness.[23]

Deng seemed to be warning that opponents of reform might try to take advantage of any complications resulting from premature reforms.

One Chinese writer explained how bureaucrats trembled at hearing the word democracy:

Democracy is regarded as a weapon to be used by the subordinates and the masses against the higher-ups and the cadres, a force to weaken and shatter stability and unity, and even something equivalent to anarchy. From this perspective, a very small number of leaders will feel frightened whenever they hear of democracy. Those leaders who are accustomed to patriarchal behavior would take any expression of different opinions as a sign of rebellion and put any convenient political label upon those who voice them.

This mentality, to a great degree, results from one's regard for his own power (actual gains or losses). In such a case, it is very difficult to persuade people with logic to cast off this mentality.[24]

One locus of institutionalized resistance to reform may be in the party's Central Discipline Inspection Commission, headed by octogenarian Chen Yun. He has focused attention on the ideological and moral qualities of party members as well as on outright corruption.[25] This provides a strong base from which to attack radical reformers.

Another set of issues involves the role of the Chinese military in politics. Two problems are paramount. First, the military may have shared the viewpoint with some top party leaders that the current arrangements are perfectly fine. They have status, nice apartments, access to cars, and other perks. Why rush into change?

The close relationship between the party and the military comes from history. In the revolutionary period, party and military were intertwined. Senior party and military leaders had deep personal relationships tempered in battle. Now this relationship is symbolized by peculiar institutional arrangements. The supreme leadership of the military is the Military Affairs Commission, a party institution. The head is Deng Xiaoping. He has given up other formal roles but retains this one, highlighting its importance. The minister of defense is subordinate to the party commission, and not really in charge of the military. Moreover, people with military backgrounds constitute a large portion of votes in the Central Committee of the Communist Party. Military people are an integral element in the political system; there is no sharp distinction between civilian and military elements in the political system. Thus, the military can make its viewpoint felt directly in the party.

A somewhat different potential problem is that the military could intervene in politics if there were the appearance of political weakness and chaos. Throughout Chinese history, when the central political system gave the appearance of being weak, local people with military power assumed greater power. "Warlordism" was a recurrent phenomenon. After the communists won the revolution in 1949, the People's Liberation Army played a critical role in civil administration for several years. To a certain extent, the cultural revolution demonstrated continuity of this tradition. When the party lost its unity, chaos broke out and regional military commanders imposed their own order. The military became a crucial element in the structure of political power at the end of the 1960's. Revolutionary committees always had a leading member from the military.

Again, after Mao died in 1976, the military played an important political role. Top central military leaders (such as Ye Jianying) contributed to the crucial decisions in arresting the "Gang of Four." Regional military leaders disarmed and controlled the gang's regional supporters, particularly in Shanghai.[26] It should be noted, however, that the military has been politically important only when it has been closely associated with core party leaders. When Defense Ministers Peng Dehuai and Lin Biao made bids for power in 1959 and 1971, they both failed.

For the future, a serious breakdown of civil order is unlikely but not completely inconceivable. If widespread student demonstrations were to occur at a time of economic stagnation, anger over inflation of food and rent prices, and if there were a lack of consensus in the central leadership, widespread disorder would be possible. China has not seen formal martial law, but it should be remembered that when Poland experienced a breakdown of civil order, a loss of political legitimacy, and the risk of a Soviet invasion, its military did impose martial law.

Robert Dahl has argued that the contesting of political issues in public is crucial for the emergence of democracy.[27] Can this occur in China without giving the appearance of that dreaded word in Chinese political culture, "chaos"? Can Chinese argue publically and not have unity, but still not give the appearance of a weakening of the central authority and without giving central and/or regional military leaders an excuse to intervene in politics?

Military leaders also have personal and institutional reasons to be dubious of the reform program. Members of the military have not benefited from the economic reforms. From 1977 to 1984, the military budget declined, both as a percentage of the national budget and in terms of absolute allocations. Moreover, when rural collective institutions were dissolved, families of military members lost the institutional base of their financial support. In addition, people in the military have not had the same opportunities to "get rich" as many others in China. Military pay scales have been frozen, as farmers' and workers' incomes have been rising. A certain amount of discontent probably exists in the military.

In 1984 China began a program to reduce its four-million-man military establishment to three million. If satisfactory alternative employment is not found for demobilized troops, another source of potential discontent will be created.

In addition the military has been going through a complex reorganization from the old field army system to a group army system. The new organization is designed to provide better coordination between specialized military units with modern technology.[28] The old commanders, lacking competence in modern technology, were probably squeezed out in this reorganization, and may be unhappy.

The military has been required to convert some production facilities to civilian use, and to make a profit. Munitions plants are now producing pots, pans, and bicycles. The partial conversion of the air force into a passenger airline is another example. The military has also been urged to compete in export markets to earn foreign exchange. Some military leaders resist the idea that they must compete economically in domestic and foreign markets and show a profit.

Many outside observers believe that military leaders in particular were dubious about Hu Yaobang's leadership qualifications. They blamed him for "putting money first," and for a moral breakdown in society. They feared a loss of military discipline as international exchanges expanded.[29]

When Hu was deposed in January 1987, some people considered this reflected enlarged influence of military leaders.[30]

Another potential obstacle is the conservative forces in the internal Public Security Bureau, with perhaps a million employees. They have energetically arrested and imprisoned political dissidents, religious figures, Western journalists, and others, from time to time.[31] Such practices are deeply embedded in the organizational culture of such systems. In the Soviet Union, of course, the zealous efforts of the KGB to smash the dissident movement removed opportunities for dialogue on political reform. In China, both reformers and the government have been careful to avoid such a polarization of views. The memories of the cultural revolution help people realize the potential costs of such polarization.

These very sensitive issues of the role of the military and internal security forces in politics are not discussed in the open press, but are on the minds of many Chinese.

## CHINESE GRIDLOCK

Another problem must also be considered. Reform inevitably is a very complicated process, affecting the interests of many people and groups in complex ways. The old system of state control of the economy and personal life was very well integrated. Reform in one area alone would not work, and would cause many other problems. Moreover, many people benefited from the system of planning and would lose these benefits if a market-oriented policy were adopted. They have resisted reform. The various interests that benefit from the current systems have been able to block change, in a manner similar to "gridlock" in Western democracies. It naturally will take time to sort out this complex combination of administrative problems and political interests, and secure each group's assent to reform.

The program of giving responsibility to a factory manager has been discussed above. The key issue is to whom would the manager be responsible? Chinese regulations were ambiguous.[32] Ultimately, the question of the responsibility of a factory manager boiled down to the question of who actually owned productive assets. On such a question, it was difficult to avoid fundamental ideological questions. In China the capital initially came from the government. Should the director be responsible to the government? If so, what incentives will there be for managers and workers? Alternatively, if the factory becomes autonomous or responsible to the workers, there effectively would have been a transfer of public assets to individuals. This had to raise many thorny problems.

China's solution to this was to allow, in 1986, small-scale production and commercial units to be given, leased, or sold to individuals. Stocks, shares, and bonds were also sold to spread the ownership of assets.

When the factory manager was given full power and responsibility to manage the factory, the Chinese recognized that some countervailing force was needed to prevent his gaining excessive power. The January 1987 directives created workers' congresses at enterprises to provide a new method of worker input. Of course, the issue of workers' participation has long been a topic of discussion in China, but apparently early modalities were judged inadequate. There have also been discussions about new tasks for the unions. Unions have been under government control. They provide some welfare functions and organize vacation trips. They help management enforce labor discipline. They have not been independent representatives of the workers. Now under discussion is the possibility of unions representing workers in contract negotiations.[33]

Establishing labor markets also presented many issues. Under faltering market conditions, would an enterprise be able to reduce its labor supply? Could old workers be laid off? This was a major problem. The "iron rice bowl" (permanent, lifetime employment) had long been considered a natural right. Chinese workers liked the idea of efficiency, but also liked their relaxed work schedules, and the freedom from fear of being fired. They resisted giving up this security. The Chinese press acknowledged that "some people are apprehensive that implementation of the labor contract system will injure the interests of workers."[34] Some even argued that China was moving into capitalist wage labor.[35]

Values appear to be changing on such issues. A large survey of state functionaries, technicians, engineers, and workers showed that over 55 percent believed that the permanent employment system failed to bring people's initiative into full play and should therefore be abolished. Of those surveyed, 87 percent considered it was reasonable to fire unqualified employees.[36]

Complicating matters was the fact that much urban housing had been financed by work units for their employees. Would a fired worker be pushed out of his housing? So far, there are few precedents because so few people have been fired.

The problem is especially intense because of subsidies built into the assignment of housing. Chinese researchers estimated that the average rent in urban China is 0.13 yuan per square meter. A detailed survey showed that the "ordinary, city, household of four" had an average of 26.13 square meters (283 square feet) of floor space. Total family income was estimated at 190 yuan.[37] At the figures given, they would pay a rent of about 3.4 yuan per month, not quite 2 percent of total family income. The rent that is paid does not cover even one-half the cost of maintenance, much less any contribution to the capital cost of housing.[38] Obviously, in such circumstances, everyone wants more subsidized housing space.

Chinese reformers proposed to stop subsidizing housing and other services through profits of the work units. Instead wages and salaries could be increased, and a housing market could be established that would not involve subsidies. One Chinese writer said, "Housing should be commercialized to replace the old housing distribution system, which is essentially a social welfare program. To begin with, the low rents should be raised."[39]

In fact, experiments were done in the fall of 1986 in a few cities to test ways of establishing such a market. (The test cities are Yantai in Shandong, Tangshan in Hebei, Changzhou in Jiangsu, Bengbu of Anhui, and Jiangmen of Guangdong.) The basic idea was for Chinese to make monthly installment payments toward purchasing their apartments. In some tests, urban residents were offered the option of making monthly payments of three times or more over their normal rents to establish ownership. In fact, even this program did not cover what the government estimated the value of apartments to be; it was thought that these payments would cover only one-third of the cost of housing, so the state was adding an additional subsidy toward the true purchase price. This program was not popular. Generally, most people in the experimental areas preferred to pay a very low rent, rather than make larger contributions toward ownership. To make this option less attractive, it was urged that rental rates be raised to a level that accurately reflected the actual costs of providing housing. In Yantai, a city where a critical experiment was attempted, rents were raised almost ten times, to 1.17 yuan per meter. This would cost the average family around 27 yuan extra each month. Special housing subsidies of 23.5 percent of wages were offered to those who signed up for the program right away. In the future, people would have to buy housing, paying 30 to 70 percent down, without subsidy.[40] Some writers suggested fixing housing prices at 200 yuan per square meter, or about 1,200 yuan per capita, a large but not completely unmanageable sum.[41]

It was assumed that commercialization of the housing system would arouse broader participation in housing construction and management. Was China contemplating private real estate entrepreneurs?[42]

This housing issue had the potential of being highly explosive. Not to reform the housing system meant continuing serious impediments to the development of the housing industry, and making job mobility more complicated. On the other hand, raising rents to appropriate levels could create a political crisis. Even if salaries were raised a commensurate amount, there would be much resentment of the increase in housing prices. In reality, people would experience a substantial increase in their equity holdings, but they would still resent higher rental charges. Despite these problems, the Central Committee approved the Yantai plan in principle. If a three month trial period were successful, it was scheduled for implementation in other areas of the country after April 1987.

Additional prerequisites for a labor market were unemployment insurance and changing the system of health benefits and pension rights so they could be detached from specific work units. Experiments were conducted on these problems.

While Chinese workers may have supported the abstract idea of reform, they did not want to live in a perfectly free market environment. They wanted to keep at least some of their accustomed social welfare benefits, including basic security of livelihood.

The other side of a labor market is freedom to seek employment. Again, there were interesting problems. With regard to college graduates, in the past, one reason for compulsory job assignments was the fact that college tuition was free, and scholarships were an integral element of student finance. Now, if the government renounced its right to assign graduates, why should it provide free education? Should students be required to pay for their education? China adopted as an interim measure a system that if a company wanted to hire a student who was not assigned there, the company would reimburse the state for tuition. There were new plans to charge tuition for college education. While students and their families might be happy to see the assignment system dropped, their parents probably considered it most unfair to have to pay for tuition. Not yet clear was what assistance would be given to students from poorer families.

In Shenzhen from December 14 to 17, 1986, students demonstrated with sporadic violence, focusing on this issue. University officials had developed and were forced to withdraw an unusual plan that would have raised tuition from a nominal 20 yuan to as much as 750 yuan. The tuition fee was to be linked to grades. A top ranked student would pay tuition of only 50 yuan, but students with low grades would be charged up to 750 yuan. Additional fees would be levied on students asking to retake exams.[43] Students at Shenzhen University are especially concerned about grades because they are not guaranteed jobs upon graduation, but have to find their own jobs.[44] For a university to have a budgetary interest in lower grades would cause student anxiety anywhere! Only a very inexperienced university management would have made this obvious mistake.

What about freedom of internal migration? Despite all the programs for expanding market relations, controls were maintained on rural residents migrating to major cities for work. At best, men could become "guest workers" with no chance of having their wives and children join them. This may seem unfair and economically inefficient, but urban residents considered these controls appropriate to prevent already crowded cities from being swamped by new migrants, as has happened in India, Mexico, and most Third World countries. Eventually, if a housing market is established, the high price of urban living space could replace administrative controls as the means to regulate urban migration and as a way to increase the attractiveness of smaller towns. But this hardly seems a big advantage now to urban residents.

Of course if enterprises could flourish under an open market, they could also collapse. Would enterprises be allowed to go bankrupt, rather than receive perpetual subsidies from the government? What would happen to the workers and enterprise assets in such a case? For a year, China has been fascinated with the implications of one experimental bankruptcy. It is touted as a sign of progress, but obviously is a frightening harbinger of the future.

Before bankruptcy could be allowed, many other reforms were needed. Unemployment insurance and social security were needed to protect workers from the incompetence of their managers. Also, to ensure that unprofitability of an enterprise truly reflected bad management, it was necessary to have prices rationalized, and to remove or equalize subsidies, windfall profits, and heavy expenses that were not related to efficiency at the present time, such as heavy pension costs for older enterprises.[45] All this takes time.

Other problems arose in the salary system. In the present system, incomes are fairly equal, but administrative means are used to ensure that China's leaders get suitable perks. Color televisions are often rationed. Soft seats on trains are available only to people above a certain rank (or foreigners). People with certain positions can use certain shops that have high quality merchandise and low prices. Should incomes be raised instead, and special goods and services be placed on the open market? People would not tolerate paying high enough salaries to government workers to compete on the open market for perks against China's new generation of businessmen. Government officials probably would also prefer having low salaries but generous perks allocated administratively. This way it is easier to obscure their high standard of living.

The reform of enterprise management also had a large impact on government finance. If factories no longer turned over profits automatically to the government, a new tax system was needed. To assure that enterprises could compete on an equal basis, a clear legal system was needed.

Expanding market interactions and competition were not welcomed by some of China's monopolistic enterprises. A fascinating example of the way established interests could create obstacles for reform came from the airline industry. China has had basically one domestic airline, Civil Aviation Administration of China. In recent years, China has encouraged the creation of regional airlines to add competition to the air system. The regional airlines, however, encountered serious problems in obtaining spare parts to service their airplanes, hiring pilots and other personnel, obtaining landing rights at the regular airports, obtaining office space for their ticket offices, and even printing their tickets in a way that clearly specifies the airline and the airport.[46]

In rural areas reforms were popular, but people had some problems. Inflation in the prices of fertilizer, machinery, and other inputs were so great in some cases that net income per acre of farmland was declining.[47]

All these problems in implementing reforms were particularly thorny because they involved taking away from people some right or privilege that they had come to take for granted. Naturally they resisted. One solution was to phase in changes gradually. Starting on October 1, 1986, new workers did not automatically have lifetime employment, but instead received fixed-term contracts. Young adults entering the labor market no longer can inherit their fathers' jobs. China's young generation will live much more in a market economy. Of course there will be problems and tensions in having young and old workers function in different economic systems, and this problem can last for several decades. But this approach has the advantage of political feasibility. Already, to a large degree, China's younger generation lives in a different cultural world from the older generation, so it should be possible to it to live under different economic arrangements also.

## MARKET FAILURE

Another problem with reform comes from the fact that in certain cases, the expansion of free markets can create new inefficiencies and problems. In economic theory, this is known as the problem of market failure. In the West, the ways free markets create problems in the agricultural sector are well understood, and in fact agriculture in most countries is highly regulated.

In China, reform began in the agricultural sector, and has been successful and popular. There has been growth in agricultural production and farm income.[48] Nevertheless, many problems are appearing, which may eventually require new regulations of market activities.

Investment in agriculture by the state and farm families is declining. There is also a reduction in the use of mechanization and irrigation. There have been shortages in supply of fertilizer and other inputs and increases in their prices of 20–40 percent. The network for supplying inputs is in tatters. Grain production declined in 1985 but rebounded in 1986. Livestock raising is suffering from the high price of animal feed, animal epidemics, and the lack of fodder processing equipment. The agricultural extension network is weak, and there is a great need to update agricultural technology knowledge. Some of the problems are caused by the fact that farmers still fear a shift in policy back to the left. They fear that they will be criticized in the future as capitalists. Moreover, they have only temporary rights to use farmland for another 7–10 years, in most cases. They do not have permanent ownership rights. They are therefore reluctant to make investments in agriculture. Environmental problems continue to expand. Desertification continues to despoil regions with fragile ecologies. Rural pollution is a new, acute problem, as rural industries spring up, and as use of agricultural chemicals is expanded.[49] Of course many of these problems are the typical problems of agriculture throughout the world.

To ensure farmers do not neglect grain in favor of cash crops, the government is stepping in by selling to them at subsidized prices 6 kg of fertilizer and 3 kg of diesel oil for each 100 kg of grain contracted for government purchase.[50]

Somewhat analogous problems are arising in the industrial sector. As enterprises function more in an open market, problems are occurring in safety, health, and environment controls. Higher profits can often be made by cutting these corners. Buildings collapse because of bad materials, design, and construction. Adulterated foods are sold.[51]

In theory, the solutions to many of these problems are clear, but for each problem, new institutional arrangements and personnel are needed. China in fact began experimenting in most of these areas. It started to train people, and tried to convince lower level managers to follow new principles and procedures. Inspection agencies are being expanded. Implementing these types of changes naturally takes time, particularly in China, which for thousands of years has recognized the rule of man, not the rule of law.

Many Chinese were also dubious about reform policies that were integrating China with the global system. Unchecked purchases of foreign goods led to a sharp drop in foreign exchange reserves. Export-oriented projects were encountering difficulty in earning foreign exchange in a competitive, stagnant world marketplace. Corrupt practices were becoming widespread. Some Chinese leaders, including politbureau member Hu Qiaomu, were criticizing the policy of openness to the outside as allowing a renewal of old imperialism.[52] It was clear that arguments about the policy of reform were continuing at the highest levels.

Dong Fureng, an economist, has detailed many of the problems and obstacles in structural reform:

In general, the public approves of the reform and wishes it success. But time and again one hears complaints and disgruntled remarks. Many factors explain this...[T]he intrusion of reform upon vested interests understandably draws complaints or dissatisfaction from some people.

...In another case, a few people's fortunes have grown so much that the gap between people's income becomes ever-widening. This also draws resentment from those who are relatively poor.

People have expected too much of the reform, only to become disappointed when it gives them less material gains than they have unrealistically anticipated. Again they complain.

In addition, interests brought by the reform whet people's appetite for more. . . . When this appetite for more is not satisfied, they begin complaining. . . .

In the reform, part of the pay rises are offset by price rises. People become resentful, even though their actual incomes increase despite the price rises. . . .

Some have lived very comfortably from the iron rice bowl. When they are pressed to work harder so as to be rewarded more, they resent the additional effort. . . .

If these complaints are given a free rein, they will snowball. In the end, they could have a negative impact on the reform, dampen people's enthusiasm and hinder the leadership in formulating policies for further reform.

[W]e should especially avoid rashly starting a reform project and then randomly scrapping it, which makes the people who have savored the benefits the project brought them very frustrated.[53]

All these problems added to opposition to reform. By late 1986, China was at a crossroads. One writer, Sun Xiaoliang, laid out the dilemma very clearly:

There are two choices concerning the speed of the reform: to accelerate or slow it. The former is indeed risky but the latter is even more risky.

In the past seven years, the aspects of management systems that are comparatively easy to handle have been reformed. What is involved in the next steps are more difficult and risky items such as pricing systems, taxes, finance, banking and investment. So far no breakthroughs have been made.

We should keep in mind that it is more risky to stop or slow the reform. The co-existence of the old and new management systems will inevitably cause economic disorder and leave room for malpractice. The reform is a boat sailing against the current and must forge ahead or it will be driven back by age-old concepts and ideas.

Also, if the new system fails to dominate over time, it will produce a socio-psychological effect causing people to lose enthusiasm for and confidence in the reforms . . .[54]

It is clear that many people were opposed to rapid reform, for many reasons. Many middle-level cadres had theoretical reservations about reform. An article in the September issue of the Communist Party's theoretical journal, *Red Flag*, carried a somber warning against absolute freedom and asserting that socialism had finally made it possible for most people to have freedom.[55] Personal interests of the bureaucrats made them fear rapid reform. Among urban factory workers, the reforms were double-edged, offering benefits but extracting a large price.

Among the general population, traditional culture asked for stability, not for democracy. Everyone was sensitive to the immediate costs of reform, and not clear about the potential long-term benefits.

In earlier years, these opponents to reform had placed limits on change. The Democracy Wall Movement was ended in 1981. In late 1983, the "anti-spiritual pollution campaign" threatened reform, but was stopped before it went very far. As reform programs advanced, however, opponents of rapid, radical reform also strengthened. In 1986, if China could have voted on reform, the nays would have gathered many votes.

A Chinese article in September 1986 nervously explained the problem:

On the one hand, political structural reform will inevitably bring about effects on people's material interests, lifestyle, concept of value, human relations as well as their ways of association. Ideological turbulence in all social strata and sections is inevitable ... We should correctly and appropriately handle the differences between all social sectors in the course of reform ... so as to *avoid major disturbances and conflicts* in the overall situation of reform.[56] (emphasis added)

Deng himself, for all his emphasis on reform, was well aware of the obstacles. He commented during fall 1986:

Some people in the party and the state are against reform, but there are not many who really oppose it.... Since our country is very large and the situation is very complicated, reform is not easy.... Therefore, we must be prudent when making policy decisions.... It will be impossible to set forth a policy for comprehensive reforms at the 13th National Party Congress, because there is not enough time; ... Because we lack experience in this regard, we are still groping our way forward.[57]

The reform movement faced a deep dilemma. Implementation of democratic reforms would have given more power to those who opposed reform. This was seen in the protracted discussions about the bankruptcy bill in the National People's Congress. On the one hand, reformers wanted to strengthen the congress. On the other hand, they wanted the law passed. There was no simple solution to this problem. Refusal to take seriously the concerns of opponents to reform would be non-democratic and self-defeating in the long run. These tensions about reform set the stage for demonstrations in December 1986 and the conservative reaction of January 1987.

These various opponents of reform resisted political change throughout the fall, and moved decisively in January 1987, as will be reviewed in the next chapters.

## NOTES

1. Mancur Olson, *The Rise and Decline of Nations: Economic Growth, Stagflation, and Social Rigidities* (New Haven: Yale University Press, 1982).

2. Lucian Pye, *The Spirit of Chinese Politics* (Cambridge, MA: MIT Press, 1968), p. 33. Richard Solomon, *Mao's Revolution and the Chinese Political Culture* (Berkeley: University of California, 1971).

3. Peter Moody, "The Romance of the Three Kingdoms and popular Chinese political culture," *Review of Politics*, 37:2 (April 1975), pp. 175–199.

4. Lucian Pye, *The Dynamics of Chinese Politics* (Cambridge, MA: Oelgeschlager, Gunn & Hain, 1981), pp. 137–38.

5. Zeng Shiping, "On reforming the foundation of China's political institutions," *Political Research*, no. 1 (1986), pp. 26–34. Available in Benedict Stavis (ed.), "Reform of China's political system," *Chinese Law and Government*, 20:1 (Spring 1987).

6. David Raddock, *Political Behavior of Adolescents in China: The Cultural Revolution in Kwangchow* (Tucson: University of Arizona Press, 1977).

7. Vitaly A. Rubin, *Individual and State in Ancient China* (New York: Columbia University Press, 1976), p. 117.

8. Jong Jian, in *China Daily* (Dec. 19, 1986), p. 4.

9. Yao Shing-mu, "Writer Bo Yang on 'Weaknesses of Chinese Culture,' " *Hong Kong Standard* (March 11, 1987), p. 7; FBIS (March 11, 1987), p. K 10.

10. William Theodore de Bary, *The Liberal Tradition in China* (New York: Columbia University Press, 1973), pp. 2, 81, 89, 101.

11. Ibid., pp. 95–98.

12. Li Kejing, "China's political restructuring . . . ," p. 13.

13. Andrew Nathan, "A factionalism model of CCP Politics," *China Quarterly*, no. 53 (Jan.-March 1973), pp. 34–66.

14. Pye, *The Dynamics of Chinese Politics*.

15. Lucian Pye, "On Chinese pragmatism," *China Quarterly*, no. 106 (June 1986), pp. 207–234.

16. Su Shaozhi, "The precondition for reform of political institutions is getting rid of feudal pernicious influences," *People's Daily* (Aug. 15, 1986). Available in Benedict Stavis (ed.), "Reform of China's political system," *Chinese Law and Government*, 20:1 (Spring 1987).

17. "Huan Xiang calls attention to the great harm of overestimating the maturity of the socialist system," *World Economic Herald* (Sept. 29, 1986), p. 1; FBIS (Oct. 14, 1986), p. K 7.

18. Jong Jian, in *Theoretical Research Bulletin*, cited in "What they are saying," *China Daily* (Dec. 19, 1986), p. 4.

19. Louise do Rosario, "The poster protesters," *Far Eastern Economic Review* (Dec. 25, 1986), p. 10.

20. Li Kejing, "China's political restructuring . . . ," p. 11.

21. Yan Mei-ning, "Further comments on Hu," *Hong Kong Standard* (Feb. 8, 1987), p. 9; FBIS (Feb. 9, 1987), p. K 5.

22. Lo Ping, "Notes on a northern journey—Deng Xiaoping criticizes Chen Yun at meeting," *Zheng Ming*, no. 108 (Oct. 1, 1986), pp. 8–12; FBIS (Oct. 9, 1986), p. K 16.

23. "China firm in continuing its reform, says Deng," *China Daily* (Dec. 13, 1986), p. 1.

24. Li Honglin, "How to make socialist democracy a reality," *World Economic Herald* (June 2, 1986). Available in Benedict Stavis (ed.), "Reform of China's political system," *Chinese Law and Government,* 20:1 (Spring 1987).

25. "Discipline Inspection Departments must act as an important force in promoting reform," *People's Daily* (Oct. 8, 1986), p. 1; FBIS (Oct. 14, 1986), p. K 1.

26. Millicent Anne Gates and E. Bruce Geelhoed, *The Dragon and the Snake* (Philadelphia: University of Pennsylvania Press, 1986), p. 144.

27. Robert Dahl, *Polyarchy* (New Haven: Yale, 1971).

28. Xu Jingyu, "All Chinese armies are turned into group armies," *Liaowang Overseas,* no. 40 (Oct. 6, 1986), pp. 16–17; FBIS (Oct. 15, 1986), p. K 11.

29. Lo Ping, "Disputes inside the party between the faction which wants Deng to stay and the faction which wants Deng to retire," *Zheng Ming,* no. 110 (Dec. 1, 1986), pp. 6–8; FBIS (Dec. 4, 1986), p. K 9.

30. Wang Bingzhang, "Cause and consequence," *China Spring Digest* (March/April, 1987), pp. 39–41. Lo Ping, "The truth of the Hu Yaobang incident," *Zheng Ming,* no. 112 (Feb. 1, 1987), pp. 6–10; FBIS (Jan. 29, 1987), p. K 6.

31. James Seymour, *China Rights Annals,* no. 1 (Armonk, NY: M. E. Sharpe, 1985), pp. 38–47, 147–175.

32. "Regulations governing the work of factory directors of state-owned industrial enterprises (Sept. 15, 1986)," *NCNA* (Feb. 5, 1987); FBIS (Feb. 5, 1987), pp. K 19–25.

33. "New trade union law is to be issued," *China Daily* (Nov. 18, 1986), p. 3.

34. "Minister of labor and personnel interviewed on the labor contract system," *People's Daily* (Oct. 5, 1986), p. 2; FBIS (Oct. 10, 1986), p. K 10.

35. Wang Jianxin, "Several questions about understanding the labor system reform," *Ban Yue Tan,* no. 18 (Sept. 25, 1986), pp. 17–19; FBIS (Oct. 10, 1986), p. K 12.

36. "Workers desire flexibility in jobs," *China Daily* (Jan. 5, 1987), p. 3.

37. "Trial housing programme tested," *Beijing Review* (Aug. 17, 1987), p. 5. *State Statistical Bureau, People's Republic of China, A Survey of Income and Household Conditions in China* (Beijing: New World Press, China Statistical Information and Consultancy Service Centre, 1985), pp. 188–190.

38. "New housing experiment being tried," *China Daily* (Dec. 31, 1986), p. 4.

39. Ibid.

40. "Trial housing programme tested," *Beijing Review* (Aug. 17, 1987) p. 5.

41. Zhang Ping, "States planning home ownership drive," *China Daily* (Nov. 11, 1986), p. 3.

42. "Apartment for every household promised," *China Daily* (Jan. 5, 1987), p. 1.

43. "Shenzhen student violence overturns higher fees plan," *South China Morning Post* (Dec. 18, 1986), p. 1.

44. "Student's independent attitudes," *China Daily* (Jan. 23, 1987), p. 4.

45. "NPC again mulls revised draft of bankruptcy law," *China Daily* (Nov. 17, 1986), p. 1.

46. "Local airlines' problems," *China Daily* (April 2, 1987).

47. Ling Zhijun and Yang Jun, "Shenxian County endeavors to find out the people's demands, sets up service companies to promote reform," *People's Daily* (Oct. 3, 1986), p. 1; FBIS (Oct. 10, 1986), p. K 19.

48. Benedict Stavis, "Some initial results of China's new agricultural policies," *World Development*, 13:12 (Dec. 1985), pp. 1299–1305.

49. "Initiative the key to farm problems," *China Daily* (March 30, 1987), p. 4. "Anhui faces problems over grain production," *China Daily* (April 1, 1987), p. 1. "Poisoning cases on rise," *China Daily* (April 3, 1987), p. 3. "Environmental crisis growing," *China Daily* (April 9, 1987), p. 4.

50. Nie Lisheng, "Farmers to receive production increases," *China Daily* (Nov. 24, 1986), p. 3; FBIS (Nov. 25, 1986), p. K 8.

51. "Poisoning cases on rise," *China Daily* (March 31, 1987), p. 3.

52. Huan Guocang, "China's opening to the West," *Problems of Communism*, 35:6 (Nov./Dec. 1986), pp. 59–77. Joseph Fewsmith, "Special Economic Zones in the PRC," *Problems of Communism*, 35:6 (Nov./Dec. 1986), pp. 78–85.

53. "Explanation eases the path of reform," *China Daily* (Jan. 19, 1987).

54. "Big risk in slowing reforms," *China Daily* (Jan. 13, 1987), p. 4.

55. "CPC top leadership is preparing public opinion for political freedom," *Ming Pao* (Oct. 26, 1986); FBIS (Oct. 29, 1986), p. K 5. Lo Ping, "Notes on a northern journey: A Yao Wenyuan type hatchet man has gone on the stage—a dispute on the political reform between those in power and in the public," *Zheng Ming*, no. 10 (Dec. 1, 1986), pp. 9–17; FBIS (Dec. 12, 1986), p. K 11.

56. "Drawing two demarcation lines ideologically in political restructuring," *Bright Daily* (Sept. 18, 1986), p. 1; FBIS (Sept. 26, 1986), pp. K 6–7.

57. "Deng on reform of political structure," *Beijing Review*, no. 20 (May 18, 1987), pp. 14–17.

# 4

## *Student Demonstrations*

Fall of 1986 was the high tide for reform. The media were filled with discussion of reform and experiments were underway. Finally, in December, hundreds of thousands of university students throughout China took to the streets, demonstrating for democracy and human rights. According to one count, the demonstrations swept 150 campuses in at least 17 cities.[1] This type of spontaneous nationwide political expression of students was unprecedented in the People's Republic.

The demonstrations became the spark that ignited open struggle between the radical and conservative reformers among the top leadership. Within weeks of the demonstrations, Hu Yaobang, the party general secretary, was forced to resign, and Premier Zhao Ziyang took over the party. The conservatives, who had resisted reforms at the summer Beidaihe meeting and in the fall, seemed to have won Deng Xiaoping into their camp. With Deng around 82 years old, China was entering the first stages of its next succession struggle. The debate about reform became intertwined with selection of future leadership.

The demonstrations had a broader significance as well. They marked the coming of age of a new generation of Chinese, with its own distinct political culture. The precise goal of the demonstrators was ambiguous. Students were demonstrating both for the government's reform program and against the government simultaneously. Students were not satisfied with the official plan that political reform would come gradually from above to below, as a gift to the people from the party and government. Students wanted a more active role. If democracy came as a gift, it could be taken away also.

In the long run, the events of winter 1986/87 underscored some problems of political legitimacy for the communist government. Youth's pleas for fundamental political reforms were answered with lectures about the virtues of socialist democracy and about their need to become more mature and realistic. It will be hard for the political system to rebuild its legitimacy in this generation, unless the reform movement gathers new momentum.

At the higher levels of the system, there still is no well-defined method for selecting top leaders and anointing them with legitimacy. With Hu Yaobang's resignation, Premier Zhao Ziyang was appointed acting party head. This violated the principle of party-state separation, and revealed an inability to agree on the next generation of leaders. If China's political system lacks legitimacy among the younger generations, and if leaders lack institutional legitimacy, them political modernization is difficult and the possibility of complex civil strife looms in the future.

## BACKGROUND TO THE DEMONSTRATIONS

Chinese youth has a long tradition of concern for national development. They have proposed reform and demonstrated ever since the late 1800s. Young intellectuals convinced the Emperor in 1898 to attempt reforms. Later, on May 4, 1919, Beijing students demonstrated against Japanese infringements of Chinese sovereignty. The student movement of December 9, 1935, against government failure to resist Japan was another historic landmark in the development of student consciousness and action.

The Tiananmen demonstration in 1976, honoring Zhou Enlai's memory and supporting liberalization, was a renewal of this tradition. This demonstration was suppressed immediately, with some bloodshed and many jail sentences. (Later it was officially admitted that this suppression was a mistake and that the demonstrations were patriotic and just.) The Democracy Wall movement in 1979/80 was also significant. After a few months of indecision, the government arrested the leaders and put some in jail for long terms. The result was effectively to put an end to public discussions about the political system for over five years.

Nevertheless, the tradition of student and youth demonstrations was not lost. Beijing students demonstrated on September 18, 1985, ostensibly against the penetration of Japanese goods into the Chinese market and government policy toward Japan, such as inviting 3,000 Japanese youth to China. Students said the funds could better be used for China's rural development. In addition, student wall posters indicated broader desires for democracy.[2] Students in Xian and Chengdu demonstrated publicly at the same time with the same issue. Student leaders urged that demonstrations be continued on December 9, the anniversary of the 1935 student movement. However, December 9, 1985, did not see large demonstrations, due to government controls.[3] December 9 the following year would be different. Fudan University students in Shanghai have demonstrated about low student stipends. Students from Xinjiang studying in Beijing and Shanghai demonstrated in 1985 against nuclear testing in their environment, and for more regional autonomy.

In spring 1986, an unusual event emboldened students. According to a Hong Kong report, two Beijing participants in the September 18 demonstrations were arrested. The father of one was a top military officer. Convinced his son had acted legally, the father brought troops to force the Beijing Public Security Bureau to free him. Deng Xiaoping tolerated this "jailbreak." Students were inspired and felt safe from arbitrary arrest.[4]

Throughout the fall semester, 1986, there were extensive campus discussions about political reform. Lectures were organized by departments and students. Special symposia were organized for students in political studies at Fudan University and elsewhere.[5] At first I was not allowed to attend such meetings because the issue of political reform was judged an internal issue; but after a while I was. Student interest in these meetings was intense. Lecture halls were packed with hundreds of students; scores more pressed their ears to the windows from outside. The emotional level at one lecture I attended was very high. It was almost a political rally.

At the same time there were tensions about campus issues at some universities. Students at Shanxi University, Taiyuan, boycotted the student canteen because food was expensive and not good. They put up posters criticizing school authorities for poor management. At Northwest University in Xian, a dispute between graduate students and a professor ended in fisticuffs and street demonstrations. At Shandong University in Jinan, protests over food led to a hunger strike and street demonstrations.[6]

Some of these management problems at universities may have been related to the rapid expansion of higher education in China. From 1980 to 1985, the total number of students in colleges and universities increased by 50 percent, from 1.14 million to 1.70 million.[7] Another background element was the highly competitive nature of college admissions. Only about 2–3 percent of high school graduates go on to college. Only about 15 percent of those who take the college entrance examinations are admitted into college. Many of those college students had been "bookworms," with little experience in society. Many had a sense of superiority, reflecting their high performance on examinations.

One of the most articulate and radical campus spokesmen for political reform was Professor Fang Lizhi, an astrophysicist and a vice president of China Science and Technology University in Hefei, Anhui. This university had just received extensive funding from the central government to make it a world-class science and engineering university.[8] Fang was a distinguished scientist, with an extensive publication record. He had been China's youngest full professor, attended many conferences abroad, and studied at Princeton University's Institute for Advanced Studies in spring 1986. He also was known as a critical, independent thinker from the 1950s, and had been branded a rightist in 1957.[9]

In 1985 Fang began to visit Chinese universities, making political speeches. He visited Beijing and Chejiang Universities in 1985. In November 1986 he went on a remarkable speaking tour that took him to Jiaotong and Tongji Universities, East China Chemical Industry College, all in Shanghai, and Ningbo University. Students were very moved by his speeches. They recorded his talks and mimeographed and circulated them. Many newspapers interviewed Fang.[10] Rapidly, he became a hero, with a broad and enthusiastic audience. In many cases, the schools where Prof. Fang spoke became focal points for student demonstrations in December.

Fang's speeches included several messages. One of his most exciting ideas was the commonplace idea from Western political philosophy that government power inherently comes from the people. Fang said, "If the democracy we are striving for remains one that is granted only from the top, then the democracy that is practiced in our society is not the true democracy.... We should not place our hope on grants from the top leadership. Democracy granted from above is not democracy in a real sense. It is relaxation of control."[11]

However, in practice, he admitted that China lacked a democratic tradition, and still followed the traditional custom of placing hope in upright officials rather than in democratic institutions. He advocated a more vigorous, independent role for the people's congress. Marxist ideology, he argued, was still evolutionary, and could not be treated as a fixed dogma. He anticipated that China's clash with Western culture would produce good results.[12]

He vigorously advocated freedom of thought in the university setting. An astrophysicist fully familiar with the trials and tribulations of Galileo, Fang described the struggles of medieval European universities to free themselves from religious dogma and adopt a scientific perspective. This was, of course, a metaphoric challenge to Chinese intellectuals and universities to free themselves from Marxist dogma. He pursued this theme explicitly, arguing that a university should not be restrained by any ideology. Within a university community, all ideologies should be subjected to questioning and research.

Coupled with this vision of a free-thinking university was his belief that intellectuals had a special responsibility and capability for social leadership. "Obviously, the supreme authority in such a developed society is knowledge, not any particular individuals. Those who have more knowledge will get more social recognition. Therefore, intellectuals inevitably become the leading power in social progress."[13] Students and intellectuals, of course, were flattered and energized by this viewpoint. Party members, particularly those with rural roots, must have been displeased with this alternative image of social leadership.

Fang ridiculed the anti-intellectual spirit in China under Mao's leadership, especially after the anti-rightist movement of 1957 when he himself was attacked. He scorned Mao's praise of the wisdom of the uneducated, and Mao's distrust of genuine intellectuals. He urged a direct attack on these Maoist ideas, so China could be successful in modernization. By way of example, he pointed out that barbers earn higher salaries than neurologists, suggesting that society valued more highly fixing what is outside a person's head than inside.

His views of Marxism were complex. He observed that Marx made an excellent, scientific analysis of capitalism over a century ago, but that hardly could offer precise instructions for socialist systems a century later. In the field of natural sciences, he was much more negative:

I have always been opposed to the view that Marxist philosophy should become the sole theoretical guidance of everything.... We have finally realized that the guidance can only lead to erroneous outcome. It has never produced correct results. For instance, none of the so-called academic criticisms conducted since liberation proved to be correct. One hundred percent wrong. The record is really shocking.[14]

The only hope for Marxism was ambiguity and flexibility. Shenzhen, the experimental district adjacent to Hong Kong, was already very similar to capitalist Hong Kong. Fang held it up as a model for Chinese-style socialism, implying that China could evolve in a flexible way without fundamentally challenging Marxism.

Fang challenged the Communist Party. He himself had first joined the party in the mid 1950s, was expelled in 1957, and later rejoined. The party, he suggested, could be a force against the exploitation of man by man and for the abolition of privilege. Of course the party could also be a vehicle for those who wanted to become high officials and rich. He endorsed the first purpose, and urged students to join the party with such goals.

Fang also made urbane comments on social progress in Europe and North America. Capitalist countries could have substantial public ownership of means of production and advanced social welfare programs, he observed.

As for China's future, he cautioned that reform was not inevitable and could be blocked. He observed that in Iran, reform programs had been overthrown, and religious fundamentalism now ruled the country. Poland also showed how reform could fail.

Interspersed with such thoughtful comments were gratuitous insults to party leaders. He chided Premier Zhao Ziyang, who while traveling in Venice, Italy, erroneously credited Copernicus with discovering that earth was round, rather than discovering that the earth revolved about the sun. That no one in the Chinese diplomatic or press corp noticed and corrected this error was a sign of weakness of the education system, according to Fang.[15]

He bragged that he criticized publicly the deputy mayor of Beijing and Hu Qiaomu, a party ideologue. He went on to argue that China's support to intellectuals was the worst of any country in the world, save Haiti and Kampuchea.

After returning from the United States in summer 1986, Fang became even more emboldened. In his speaking tour of November 1986, he was increasingly blunt and even reckless in his comments, especially in Shanghai. At Tongji University on November 18, he said:

Socialism is at a low ebb. There is no getting around the fact that no socialist state in the post-World War II era has been successful, and neither has our own thirty-odd year long socialist experiment.... I am here to tell you that the socialist movement, from Marx and Lenin to Stalin and Mao Zedong, has been a failure.

I think that complete Westernization is the only way to modernize.[16]

He derided party ideologue Hu Qiaomu for attempting to intervene in scientific debate:

We physicists and astronomers have our own standards. What does philosophy have to do with us?... We welcome comments from [Hu Qiaomu] if you understand astrophysics, but if you don't, then get out of our way![17]

At Jiaotong University, he suggested that students were a great potential political force:

Students are a progressive force for democratization. This has been the case in all past eras... Chinese intellectuals should demonstrate their own strength. In fact, they already have this strength; but they are not conscious of it or have not dared to demonstrate it. If only they dare to stir up trouble, the impact will be very great.[18]

These comments electrified his audiences. Students throughout Shanghai and the country were fascinated by Fang's direct, nonideological comments. Because of his perspectives and values, his status as a natural scientist, and his personal courage to go on a speaking tour, he became a hero. My students were well aware of Fang's visit to Shanghai, and his comments. They read his speeches and considered him as somewhat like Andrei Sakharov in the Soviet Union, being both a dissident and a physicist.

Vice Premier Wan Li, who had governed Anhui previously, visited Prof. Fang's university on November 30 and reminded all present that "university presidents must conscientiously implement the party's line, principles, and policies.... "[19] He debated Fang and not only failed to convince the students, but antagonized them further.[20] At some confrontation with Fang, Wan Li said, "I have already granted you enough freedom and democracy." Fang reportedly hit the table and fired back, "What do you mean, enough democracy? It was the people who made you Vice Premier. It's not up to any single person to hand out democracy."[21]

Fang's comments and actions not only reflected great personal courage but implied that he had some protection from higher officials. Did Fang act spontaneously? Was he trying to head off an anticipated conservative backlash? Did he know about the opposition to reform at the Beidaihe summer meeting and later in the fall? Some students thought he was a close friend of Zhao Ziyang and Hu Qili.[22] Eventually, Fang Lizhi was removed from office and from the Communist Party (again), and became the scapegoat for the student demonstrations.

During this time period, Chinese students had inspiration from international events also. They were well aware of violent student riots in South Korea, as well as in France. They also knew that mass demonstrations had contributed to overthrowing the Marcos government in the Philippines. Chinese television nightly was showing demonstrations everywhere in the world. Probably the propaganda officials who selected news for broadcast judged that scenes of protest demonstrations in foreign countries would show that other countries were characterized by chaos. They did not realize that these broadcasts were giving students new ideas about "normal" political processes.

Students in Shanghai were further inflamed by a peculiar incident. Some Jiaotong postgraduate students in the audience of a "Jan and Dean" rock 'n roll concert on December 9, 1986, responded to the invitation of the performers and came on the stage to dance. After the concert was over, they were taken to the stadium office and summarily beaten up by guards. There were conflicting reports on the number beaten up, ranging from one to four. There were also conflicting reports on whether they were men or women. Why did the guards beat them? The best interpretation is the simplest: guards simply assumed that any spectators coming down from stadium seats, jumping over the rail, and entering the performers' arena were violating rules. They did not understand the English language invitations to come to the stage, had never encountered this custom, and were deaf to explanations.[23]

The incident outraged students. It symbolized the gap between youth and authorities. The authorities did not understand the English language invitations, did not understand the international culture of rock concerts, and were quick to use violence to punish youth. Eventually, after several weeks, an apology was offered, soothing anger and closing the specific incident. But by then it was too late. The anger created by this incident contributed to the demonstrations that soon followed.

## CHRONOLOGY: DECEMBER 5, 1986-JANUARY 9, 1987

By December, there were enough sparks and kindling for a conflagration. Emotions and politics combined, and students took to the streets in an unprecedented manner. The demonstrations began at Fang Lizhi's China Science and Technology University in Hefei, Anhui. At a rally on December 4, Fang told his students, "Democracy is not granted from the top, it is won by individuals."[24] Fang reportedly urged students to respect the constitution; students considered this an endorsement of demonstrating.[25] The next day, roughly 1,000 demonstrated.

December 9, 1986, was the anniversary of the 1935 student movement. With this as a date to commemorate, students organized an unprecedented coordinated demonstration in three cities, Hefei, Wuhan, and Xian. Organizing was probably accomplished by telegraphing through student unions at various universities. In Hefei, roughly 3,000 students participated. They protested to local officials that the university had appointed the head of the students' union without consulting the students, much less letting students vote for their union leader. Students also wanted to nominate candidates for the provincial people's congress.[26]

In Wuhan, some 5,000 to 7,000 students from several universities also demonstrated.[27] The demonstration did not have a focused set of demands. Political concerns were important. Students were distressed by the bankruptcy of communist leadership. They felt corruption and nepotism were widespread. Opportunities for good jobs were closed to all but relatives of high leaders. Wuhan had just had local elections. Following the normal pattern of party control, the elections gave no opportunity for independent political viewpoints. This further angered students. Campus issues were also prominent. Quality and price of food, as well as rats in the dormitories were issues. Students also felt that the student union was not really representing them. While students had these types of complaints, they had few coherent positive proposals. Freedom meant fewer required courses and more flexibility in job assignments. Democracy was little more than a slogan reflecting a general affinity for things Western. Similar demonstrations took place on the same day in Xian.

News spread quickly. The shortwave broadcasts of Voice of America

(VOA) were followed avidly by students. Many students had shortwave receivers; they are encouraged to listen regularly to practice English. Shortwave news reports have been a major source of international news and perspectives for students. VOA's reports on China's student demonstrations, supplemented by reports of the British Broadcasting Corporation (BBC), became the main source of information for students, as well as for me. VOA reports were even posted on bulletin boards at Fudan, to keep students informed on late-breaking news. Students got letters from their friends at various cities a few days later, confirming the accuracy of the shortwave news reports. Not until over a week passed did Chinese media begin to cover the events.

Within a few days of the December 9 demonstrations, more student demonstrations broke out at Shandong University, Shenzhen, and Kunming. These were reactions to news of demonstrations in other cities. At Beijing University students were reported to be putting up posters calling for democracy, even though school officials were pulling them down.[28]

In Shanghai, wall posters first appeared at Jiaotong (Communications) University on December 10. This was the place where Fang Lizhi had given his bluntest criticism of socialism, and his call for complete Westernization. It was also one of the universities where students were allowed to find their own jobs, and perhaps this fact gave students a stronger sense of independence. Posters appeared at other universities in the next days, reporting information on the demonstrations in other cities. At Jiaotong, an order was given to take down the posters, and the students planned a march to protest this order.

Shanghai Mayor Jiang Zemin visited Jiaotong on Thursday, December 18. At a boisterous public meeting, he endorsed student interest in democracy, but also called for stability and unity.[29] He also asked students to cancel their planned march. Many students interrupted with heckling and questions. Finally, one student asked Mayor Jiang whether there was freedom of press in China, and whether he had been elected mayor by the people of Shanghai. Of course everyone knew that the mayor of Shanghai was appointed by the Central Committee, and was not elected. The question deftly exposed and challenged the political legitimacy of the mayor, and by implication, the whole communist system. Stunned, the mayor demanded to know the questioner's name and department. Students were outraged at this attempted intimidation. Pandemonium broke out as students protected the questioner from the mayor.[30] Other students asked whether the constitutional amendments in 1980 eliminating the right to put up posters had been approved by the Chinese people, or whether the Chinese people had actually endorsed the four cardinal principles.[31]

News of this event spread quickly to other campuses in Shanghai. On

Thursday, December 18, several hundred Tongji students paraded to Fudan, calling for liberty and democracy, and decrying bureaucracy. Thousands of Fudan students watched and eventually joined in marching to nearby Peace Park. The leaders called for larger, more formal demonstrations.

The next afternoon, Friday, December 19, students from several universities (Tongji, East China Normal University, Fudan, and others) demonstrated peacefully. They went to the Bund (the symbolic center of Shanghai along the waterfront) and City Hall (along the Bund), and then to People's Square (the site of the Shanghai People's Congress), carrying signs for democracy and human rights. All this was immediately reported to students throughout China by VOA.[32] Students wrote slogans on bed sheets, proclaiming "Freedom," "Human Rights," "We hope the Christ of Freedom will Appear," and "Against Dictatorship."

Police blocked off the square, allowing in only students with ID cards. Foreigners were kept out. Many non-students wanted to join, looking for something interesting, not understanding the students' political purposes. They disregarded the discipline of the student demonstrators. Police tried to keep them separate from students. Students were very disappointed when no representatives of the Shanghai People's Congress would come out and meet them. Over a thousand climbed the fence in front of the congress building, to escape the pressure of crowds, to get a better view, and to get closer to the building. They milled around the steps in front of the door, flourishing their signs. They were cheered by demonstrators outside the fence. Unarmed police guarded the door.

Students demanded to meet with the mayor. There was no sign of the mayor or other high officials. The sit-in began to dissipate after two hours, as students were cold and hungry. To keep the demonstration coherent, the students marched en masse back to city hall singing the "Internationale," hoping to see the mayor himself. While demonstrating, students had intense discussions about democracy with each other and with non-student demonstrators and observers. This was the first time since 1980 that there was open public discussion about reform of the political system and about practical steps toward democracy.

Students waited for hours, and finally, around 11:00 p.m., ten student representatives entered City Hall. They met first with Vice Mayor Ye Gongqi. Later Mayor Jiang came, even though he was suffering from minor head injuries from an automobile accident. Students had four demands. First, they wanted Jiang to address them. Second, they wanted the demonstration to be treated as legal and patriotic. Third, they wanted assurances that students would not be discriminated against in the future because of participation in the events. Fourth, they wanted newspapers to carry factual, fair reports about the demonstrations. The vice mayor urged calm, and offered to arrange busses for students to return to campus. Students were angry with this put-down, and continued bois-terous demonstrations after midnight. The students stayed overnight, despite bitter cold, gaining food and moral sustenance from small ped-dlers with food stands, and from other city residents. New groups of students joined in throughout the process, and some left.

The early morning hours of Saturday were critical. The demonstration in front of city hall was blocking a major terminus in the city bus routes, which would begin normal operations at 6:00 a.m. Police warned stu-dents twice to disburse and threatened to use "administrative means." Finally, around 5:45 a.m., under floodlights, police marched in to clear the area, their boots and loudspeakers leaving an indelible mark in the minds of the demonstrators. Students were forcibly removed by police, put in busses, and sent back to their campuses. Two women students first challenged the police. They and others who refused to leave received beatings by police and were detained but not formally arrested. Some students had their eyeglasses broken, and one broken leg was reported. Students in detention were treated well and offered cigarettes. Their names were registered. Throughout the whole incident, police snatched any cameras and opened them to expose the film.[33]

To protest this action, later on Saturday many tens of thousands of young people, students and non-students, and many adults demon-strated at People's Square. Slogans on the second day were "Against Police Brutality," "Release our Fellow Students," "Support Deng Xiao-ping and Support Reform," "Oppose Conservatism," "Chen Yun—Please Step Down from Power." Police allowed only students with ID cards to enter. Eager to avoid confrontation with police, students shared food with them. Police were also polite. The demonstrators divided up into groups, some going to city hall, others going elsewhere. The city hall demonstration continued well into the night. Demonstrators were careful this time not to block bus transportation.[34] This was probably the largest independent demonstration in China since the founding of the People's Republic in 1949.

Demonstrations continued Sunday. Students from Hangzhou wanted to come to Shanghai to support the demonstrations. Police there blocked the train station.[35] In Sunday's demonstrations, the government charged that 31 police were beaten up. Students ridiculed the accusation that they were responsible for violence.[36]

Student demonstrators felt a sense of exhilaration. They felt they were making a great step toward changing their country, and that they were becoming like students in other countries. For many, the political ob-jectives were very vague, but the emotional content was very deep. There was very little violence. Property destruction was limited to two vehicles being overturned by crowds led by two young workers, not by students. Windows were not broken, fires were not set, police were not attacked, and police did not riot. There were no pictures of bloody, bandaged heads, no deaths, and no funeral marches that would lead to greater violence.

In following days, Shanghai students continued to demonstrate, but in smaller numbers. Discussions on campus were intense. Of course there were many different viewpoints among students. Some were enthusiastic for reform. Some were cautious, urging care to avoid antagonizing leaders. Others were cynical. Many ignored the whole event. Some were curious spectators.

Wall posters blossomed. At Fudan University, posters included Patrick Henry's slogan, "Give me Liberty or Give me Death!" Martin Luther King's speech describing a dream of freedom and justice was posted. A *Time* magazine editorial praising the institutionalized methods available in the United States to investigate violations of law by high officials (in sending arms to Iran) was quoted. Voice of America news broadcasts were quickly transcribed and displayed. Some posters described events or listed student demands. One poster suggested adding a new verse to the Communist Internationale, calling for the creation of a democratic society with freedom and human rights. Some posters directly challenged the legitimacy of the communist government but most posters discussed the problems in China's political system along the lines of the criticisms in the official press. Some posters were in proper Chinese poetic form; others were more in graffiti style. One poster attracted attention for its clever wording, even though there was little agreement with its political message. It said: "Chairman Mao sleeps forever, Chairman Deng taxes forever, Sun Yatsen lives forever."[37]

Some posters focused on campus issues. Students wanted student unions to have more independence, and to be controlled by students rather than by the university. They also requested better food at lower prices in campus dining halls.

Student posters made virtually no reference to the Democracy Wall Movement of 1980. There was no poster saying "Free Wei Jingsheng," one of the jailed leaders of the movement. Apparently that movement and its leaders did not loom large in students' consciousness. Wei Jingsheng was active for only a brief period in Beijing, and the Chinese press did not print much about him. There is, of course, no organization in China that provides historical continuity between each episode of protest. Wei seems better known abroad than in China.

Students felt they had demonstrated enough for a while, and were realizing that their impact was limited. Communication among students on individual campuses and especially between campuses was weak, making it difficult to organize cohesive demonstrations. They had made themselves heard, but did not expect this demonstration to go much further.

On Monday, December 22, the Shanghai city government moved to end the demonstrations. It issued regulations requiring that any demonstrations needed permits that specified the location, route, and time. Of course there would be no recourse to an independent judicial determination about whether the denial of a request for a permit was unreasonable. This set the stage for a serious confrontation, because continued student demonstrations would be against the law. Police could use force to stop unlicensed demonstrations. Moreover, a state education commission official reminded everyone that the right to put up wall posters did not have constitutional protection.[38] (The constitutional provision protecting this freedom had been amended away in 1980, as part of the termination of the democracy wall movement.) The implication of this comment was that posters on campuses could be torn down and banned at any time.

On Tuesday, a few hundred Tongji students marched from campus to downtown and back, with banners and a cooperative police escort. Student marshals assured that peaceful discipline would be maintained and that non-students would be excluded from this parade. Shanghai city officials later met with 5,000 students at Tongji University. Students demanded that their demonstration be considered patriotic and just, and that there be no punishments. They also asked for access to the press.[39]

Students were sensitive to the possibility of violence and the appearance of contributing to chaos. Demonstrations reminded many people of the onset of the cultural revolution, and this brought on negative feelings. The analogy was flawed; the 1986 demonstrations were basically spontaneous, while the cultural revolution was incited by the highest leaders. Despite such differences, the memory and lessons of the cultural revolution were deep: stability was very important but somewhat fragile. Anything that threatened to lead to chaos was to be avoided. Students also did not want to antagonize Shanghai's citizens with traffic disruptions. They realized that many citizens in Shanghai did not perceive democracy to be an urgent need.

Students also had to return to studying for final exams. They worried whether active participation in student demonstrations might result, upon graduation, in a work assignments to undesirable units, or in remote locations. All demonstrations had been videotaped by the police, making it relatively simple for university officials to know the activities of individual students. Students in Shanghai curtailed demonstrations, at least for a while.

As students in Shanghai went back to classes, 5,000 students in Beijing demonstrated on Tuesday, December 23, in support of Shanghai students.[40] In Nanjing, students demonstrated for four days, from December 22 to 25.[41] In these demonstrations, the main demands were for more democracy, less autocracy and bureaucracy, and an independent student association. Students also protested against a mandatory examination of political (Marxist) theory. Both students and police tried to avoid violence, but there were scattered incidents of damage to cars and shops, and some small fires. Bus transportation was disrupted.[42] At first, Nanjing students' demands focused on campus issues, and then gradually enlarged, including the right to elect their own student union, freedom of press, and eventually democracy and human rights. Students in Nanjing were not trying to overthrow the government, but were trying to make heard their concerns about the slowness of political reforms.[43]

Students in Tianjin demonstrated on Wednesday.[44] Roughly 3,000 demonstrators tried to push their way through a police cordon around a government building. Several were hurt in the melee. Some posters reminded students of the mass movement in the Philippines to overthrow Marcos and suggested that could serve as a model for their own struggle.[45] Students in Guangzhou, Hangzhou, and Suzhou also demonstrated. This type of nationwide, spontaneous movement was unique in the years since the revolution of 1949.

At Fudan, the conclusion of the tumultuous week was graceful. The campus mood turned festive with dance parties on Christmas eve. The next morning, wall posters were taken down by university janitorial staff. A *People's Daily* editorial stressed that reform would be a gradual process, carried out under the party's leadership. "A long process is needed to build up a socialist political structure that is highly democratic, efficient and with a complete legal system. This cannot be realized overnight.... Political reform is a process of self-perfection for the socialist system, and must be conducted under the leadership of the party."[46] This phase of the mass student outpouring in Shanghai seemed suspended.

However, in Beijing, students tried to push the movement forward. They were especially annoyed at the Beijing city government for issuing on December 26 a "10-Point Temporary Regulation" for controlling and regulating demonstrations.[47] Students considered these regulations too strict and unfair. Vice Premier Wan Li visited Beijing University (date uncertain), and argued that the party was like the mother of students, and therefore could beat students to discipline them. Students angrily said they did not regard the party as a mother.[48]

On December 29, 1–3 thousand students held an early morning demonstration, in violation of city regulations. Students demonstrating at Beijing Teachers' College were not allowed off campus. At Beijing University, posters called for a New Year's Day demonstration at Tiananmen, which would also be in violation of new regulations.[49] They pushed China toward a new era of confrontation politics.

The government moved to frighten off the proposed demonstration. The day before the proposed demonstration, it formally charged several people with disrupting public order, a crime with a jail sentence. One of the people was also charged with counterrevolutionary activities. This crime has a possible death sentence. In Beijing, Xue Deyun, an unemployed worker from Guizhou, was charged with inciting students to riot. In Shanghai, Shi Guanfu, a worker in a lacquerware factory, was charged with organizing a party called Weimin (Protect People) Party, collecting weapons, and distributing leaflets inciting students to struggle against the Communist Party.[50] The implication was clear that people who persisted in illegal demonstrations in Beijing were to be treated severely.

Nevertheless, Beijing students continued their demonstrations. Thousands marched in Beijing, from the university area to downtown and along Changanjie, the broad central avenue, carrying signs saying, "Long Live Democracy." Other signs said, "Freedom to Demonstrate," and "Cancel the 10 Article Regulations."[51] Hundreds of police cordoned off the large Tiananmen plaza, but eventually demonstrators entered and stayed overnight in the snow. Finally at dawn they disbursed. The government promised to investigate who organized these illegal demonstrations.[52] Students in Wuhan demonstrated (again) on New Year's Day in response to calls from Beijing students, but heavy rains kept the demonstration small and brief.

Beijing campuses were calm thereafter, though students continued to put up "illegal" large character posters on campus.[53] On January 5, 1987, a few hundred Beijing University students had a demonstration at which copies of the *Beijing Daily* were burned, in a highly dramatic protest against inaccurate press reports.[54] Postering continued another day.

Student demonstrations ended on two strange notes. On January 8, hundreds of visiting African students studying in Beijing staged a march from the university area to the Sudanese embassy. They protested routine discrimination and a particular letter, ostensibly from the Chinese Student Association, but perhaps a forgery. The African students considered the letter racist.[55] Government officials met with representatives of the African students the next day.[56] The Chinese government could not have been happy to see demonstrations emerging as a routine method of political input, and they must have been very embarrassed diplomatically.

Another strange event closed out the demonstrations. From January 5 to 7, intense fighting was reported on the Vietnamese border. Casualties on both sides were claimed to be in the hundreds.[57] Chinese press linked the events with Vietnamese provocations on the border, but also with operations of Vietnamese troops in Kampuchea, along the Thai border, in recent days.[58] Was China "teaching Vietnam another lesson"? Would war hysteria be used to end student demonstrations? Were leaders in the Chinese military creating a new political environment? Wei Jingsheng, a leader of the Democratic Movement in 1978–1980, was eventually charged with divulging information (known to almost every-one) about China's Vietnam war of 1979, and jailed for fifteen years for this crime.

## IMPLICATIONS OF THE DEMONSTRATIONS

Among many professors and lower-level cadres, the initial reaction to the student demonstrations was surprise. At Fudan, the presumption had been that students were too busy studying and were under the control of political instructors who lived in the dormitories. Demonstrations were considered unlikely.

The unexpected did happen, and Fudan students joined the demonstrations. Many faculty were sympathetic. Certainly they supported the general principle that Chinese students should be concerned with national political issues. They felt students were basically expressing an emotional view, and did not have clearly defined political goals. They realized that the demands of the students and the content of most posters were generally reasonable and in conformity with national reform policy and comments by national leaders.

At the same time, they raised questions about tactics. Some felt that recent economic and political reforms were enough to inspire confidence. Demonstrations directly criticizing the political establishment were not appropriate at this juncture and might be counter-productive. Some of my colleagues were disturbed by disruptions to traffic in a city where normal traffic is a serious problem. Anyone who arrived home from work two hours late because of traffic disruptions would feel some hostility, especially considering the packed busses in which people would have to wait. Traffic jams could also hurt production of some enterprises near the end of the year. This problem was particularly significant because workers' wages in many enterprises were linked to whether production exceeds plans.

If non-students and workers had joined the demonstrations in large numbers, China might have faced a political crisis of major proportions, as has occurred in the past in Hungary, Czechoslovakia, and Poland. This did not happen, for many good reasons. Wages have gone up more than inflation for most workers. Even young workers, who could protest the loss of the "iron rice bowl" implicit in the new contract system of labor, appreciate the freedom of being able to shift their work, and many have very high wages. Moreover, markets were well stocked with vegetables, fruit, meat, and fish. The rapid construction of new housing is obvious. Most people felt that the government was working to solve the immediate basic economic problems.

As for a more democratic political system, most non-students probably do not think much about this issue. The nature of the political system is taken for granted. It is not something people think can be changed. Some may view democracy as a desirable goal for the distant future, but it is not considered necessary right away, and in any event can not be accepted by the political establishment. Some citizens commented to demonstrating students, with some justification, that the students already had more freedom than the rest of the population. For these reasons, the general public and especially the factory workers did not join the student demonstrations. Just to make sure they did not join, officials, at least in Shanghai, issued orders to factories forbidding workers from joining demonstrations and ordering that violators of this policy receive no pay bonuses.[59]

However, the government may have been worried about the possibility of broader participation in future demonstrations. Many citizens applauded the student demonstrators, and contributed food, money, and even sheets to make banners.[60] Inflation of food prices was quite serious, and prices were scheduled to rise more in January 1987. Inflation of food prices has been the classic spark for massive demonstrations around the world. Moreover, the plans to remove subsidies from the urban housing system and to raise sharply rental payments certainly could have brought many non-students into the streets.

Perhaps most importantly, Shanghai now had what might be called a lumpen proletariat. It was made up of many elements. For several years, the government has not assigned high school graduates to jobs. Some do not find jobs, and survive by small scale marketing, transportation, or construction. There was also a substantial, temporary migrant population in Shanghai, looking for day labor, construction work, and transport work. Many merchants and peddlers come to Shanghai with agricultural produce, handicraft products, and consumer goods. None of these people was under the watchful eye of a regular work unit, with its tight social controls. The Chinese press acknowledged, "No management departments have yet been set up to deal with the rural influx and the surplus labor force from the countryside."[61] All youth, and especially these, might find a demonstration to be something new and exciting. These people might be especially prone to disruptive violence. Some young non-student citizens did join the demonstrations for this reason.

Deng was reported by Hong Kong journalists to have been extremely worried that workers might join the students. The trade union movement in Poland flashed across his mind.[62] The two people eventually charged with inciting violence in Shanghai, namely overturning a car, were both workers. One, Wang Guishan, 28 years old, was a foundry worker. The other, Xue Wenzeng, was a bus repairman.[63] The others charged with inciting to riot or counterrevolutionary activities, as mentioned earlier, were workers or unemployed workers.[64] Officials probably feared that these people could be mobilized in the future simply for excitement. Students, under the watchful eyes of their political instructors, and fearful of their future job assignments, were not such a real worry to officials. At least one person arrested in Beijing had been involved with the earlier democracy movement.[65]

The short-term resolution of the impasse was handled gracefully. Students were able to express themselves without directly opposing the government. They did not plan or want their demonstration to be a revolution. They were supporting the party's reform program. They ended demonstrations before the government resorted to suppression, and before they lost legitimacy by creating too much disruption. Students did not want to weaken the position of Deng Xiaoping and other reformers. On campuses, they put up signs calling for support of reform and of Deng.

At the same time, the government did not get the blame for crude, violent action. Students were not beaten, much less killed. According to rumor, those few detained were released upon instructions of top leaders such as Li Peng.[66] The government avoided brutality but was not perceived as yielding to student demands. It showed no weakness and set no precedents for allowing future demonstrations. While opposing the student demonstrations, the government did not oppose the goals of political reform. It praised the students: "We would like to point out that most students demonstrated out of their concern for the reform and their good intentions to accelerate the advance of the socialist democratization. Their enthusiasm is understandable."[67]

Both students and government were sensitive to the need to avoid violence. Both sides realized that whoever was blamed for violence would lose face. In this regard, the December 1986 demonstrations were handled differently from previous large demonstrations. The previous ones were suppressed. Moreover, in Shanghai, students who had tried to establish an opposition party were executed around 1982 for undertaking counterrevolutionary activities, ostensibly because they were collecting firearms for armed struggle against the system.

The weeks of protest activity revealed much about the character of the Chinese media. During the period of demonstrations, Chinese students found the most useful, accurate source of news was the shortwave radio. Voice of America and BBC were followed carefully. One of the demands of students was that the local Chinese media cover the demonstrations. The Chinese government criticized VOA for interfering in China's domestic politics and in particular for carrying an interview with I.F. Stone, the highly independent journalist distinguished for his decades of criticism of U.S. policies. Stone had praised the Chinese students for their demonstrations for democracy. Eventually, the Chinese press did carry stories. It stressed the government reaction to the demonstrations, rather than the perspective of the demonstrators themselves. The events did not alter the perception that the press was a simple mouthpiece of the top political leaders.

In the absence of suitable newspapers, wall posters played a large role. Throngs of students read, copied, and tape recorded wall posters. They were fascinated to see the views of other students and to discover the widespread political dissent. In response, prohibitions on the use of wall posters were tightened. The Chinese press reported that wall posters were bad for socialist democracy because they were subject to abuse and slander. They could incite radical action. They intensified disagreements and wasted time. The government then emphasized the right of people to take down big character posters. "Efforts to prevent people from taking down posters are illegal."[68]

The long-term impact of the demonstrations is likely to be significant. The demonstrations shocked leadership at all levels. It became clear that China's youth had very different political values from older generations. The demonstrations were, at one level, the "coming-out" party of China's new generation.

The demonstrations will have another broader political impact also. The possibility of a challenge to communist rule in China must now be considered. Of course a serious challenge will need far better organization and leadership, and will require mass participation beyond students. This possibility places a clear limitation on the political system. It must provide continued economic growth, better living conditions, and continued reform. Otherwise, next time student demonstrations occur it could be the spark of a prairie fire, not a candle.

Others in the leadership drew another lesson. To them, it meant that reform had gone too rapidly. Demands for reform were going too far. Control and stability were threatened. They used the demonstrations as a way of slowing down reform.

## NOTES

1. Lawrence MacDonald, "Deng lends weight to anti-liberal backlash," *South China Morning Post* (Jan. 12, 1987), p. 17.

2. "Angry voice of students of Beijing University," *China Spring Digest*, 1:1 (Jan./Feb. 1987), pp. 37–43.

3. Hsiao Chang, "The cause and effect of student demonstrations in December," *Zheng Ming*, no. 111 (Jan. 1, 1987), pp. 12–13; FBIS (Jan. 5, 1987), pp. K 9–10.

4. Ibid.

5. "Summary of the symposium on political and economic restructuring," *People's Daily* (Nov. 3, 1986), p. 5; FBIS (Nov. 7, 1986), p. K 1.

6. "Student upheaval: What's it all about?" *Beijing Review*, no. 8 (Feb. 23, 1987), pp. 17–21.

7. Hu Junkai and Zhao Yining, "University students and higher education," *Beijing Review*, no. 8 (Feb. 23, 1987), pp. 21–25.

8. "Anhui Science Technology University upgraded," *NCNA* (Sept. 20, 1986); FBIS (Sept. 22, 1986), p. O 1.

9. "Fang Lizhi's Biography," *China Spring Digest* (March/April, 1987), p. 2.

10. *People's Daily* (Sept. 21, 1986), p. 3. *Anhui Daily* (Oct. 25, 1986). A speech to Beijing reporters on September 3, 1986, was published in Society (*Shehui Bao*; Oct. 28, 1986), and reprinted in *The Nineties* (Feb. 1987), pp. 52–54. *World Economic Herald* (Nov. 24, 1986), available in FBIS (Dec. 19, 1986), p. K 13. *Bright Daily* (Nov. 1986), available in *Beijing Review*, no. 50 (Dec. 15, 1986), pp. 16–17. *People's Daily* (Nov. 27, 1986), pp. 1, 4. Fang's speeches at Jiaotong University, November 15, 1986, and Tongji University, November 18, 1986, and another article are available in *China Spring*, no. 45 (March 1987), pp. 11–33. Portions of the Jiaotong speech were published as "A Chinese Tom Paine speaks out on democracy," in the *Washington Post* (Jan. 18, 1987), p. C 1. Translations of the Jiaotong and Tongji speeches are available in *China Spring Digest*, 1:2 (March/April 1987), pp. 12–25, 26–29.

11. Jiaotong speech, reported in the *Washington Post* (Jan. 18, 1987).

12. *Anhui Daily* (Oct. 25, 1986), summarized in *China News Analysis*, no. 1328 (Feb. 1, 1987), p. 6.

13. "Professor Fang Lizhi, just back from Europe," *World Economic Herald* (Nov. 24, 1986).

14. Speech at Jiaotong, reported in the *Washington Post* (Jan. 18, 1987).

15. Ge Sheng, "Fang Lizhi—a model of Chinese intellectual," *China Spring Digest* (March/April 1987), p. 9.

16. "Democracy, Reform and Modernization," Speech on November 18, 1986, at Shanghai Tongji University; *China Spring Digest* (March/April 1987), pp. 12–13.

17. Ibid.

18. "Student upheaval: What's it all about?" *Beijing Review*, no. 8 (Feb. 23, 1987), pp. 17–18.

19. "Wan Li discusses education work in Anhui," *NCNA* (Dec. 3, 1986); FBIS (Dec. 23, 1986), pp. K 18–19.

20. Nina McPherson, "Teacher faces Beijing's wrath," *South China Morning Post* (Jan. 12, 1987), p. 17. Lo Ping, "The Huangpu Jiang roars on," *Zheng Ming*, no. 111 (Jan. 1, 1987); FBIS (Jan. 8, 1987), p. K 6.

21. *Der Spiegel* (Jan. 12, 1987), pp. 100–102; FBIS (Jan. 21, 1987), p. K 13.

22. *China Spring Digest* (March/April, 1987), p. 30.

23. Lulu Yu, "Beating 'sparked rallies,'" *South China Morning Post* (Dec. 28, 1986). The Chinese press commented that the first performance was marked by very sedate audience reaction. "Shanghai rocks with U.S. band—but quietly," *China Daily* (Dec. 8, 1986).

24. "Student upheaval: What's it all about?" *Beijing Review*, no. 8 (Feb. 23, 1987), pp. 17–18.

25. Lo Ping, "The Huangpu Jiang roars on," *Zheng Ming*, no. 111 (Jan. 1, 1987); FBIS (Jan. 8, 1987), p. K 2.

26. Louise do Rosario, "The poster protesters," *Far Eastern Economic Review* (Dec. 25, 1986).

27. I visited Wuhan in early January. This paragraph reflects the views of faculty members at a university there.

28. *Voice of America* (Dec. 15, 1986).

29. "How the student demo happened," *China Daily* (Dec. 25, 1986), p. 4.

30. "Boos and hisses for the mayor," *South China Morning Post* (Dec. 24, 1986). The reporter for this Hong Kong paper talked with students in Shanghai. I heard the same story.

31. Lawrence MacDonald, "Assembly preceding Shanghai demonstrations noted," AFP (Dec. 23, 1986); FBIS (Dec. 23, 1986), p. O 2. Another account is in *China Spring* (May 1987), pp. 45–47.

32. Voice of America (Dec. 20, 1986). Lin Han-chiang, "Special dispatch from Shanghai, students' demonstrations are spontaneous, were not led by Jiaotong University student federation," *Ming Bao* (Dec. 25, 1986), p. 2; FBIS (Dec. 29, 1986), p. O 11.

33. Graphic and perhaps exaggerated accounts of violence from Tongji University wall posters are reported in *South China Morning Post* (Dec. 26, 1986). See also Lo Ping, "The Huangpu Jiang roars on."

34. BBC carried estimates of 70,000 demonstrators (Dec. 21, 1986).

35. Voice of America (Dec. 25, 1986).

36. Voice of America (Dec. 22, 23, 1986); BBC (Dec. 22, 1986).

37. "Mao Zhuxi wan shui [sleep], Deng Zhuxi wan shui [tax], Sun Zhongshan wan sui [years].

38. "It's legal if students demonstrate—official," *China Daily* (Dec. 22, 1986), p. 1.

39. Voice of America (Dec. 24, 1986).

40. Voice of America (Dec. 24, 1986).

41. Voice of America (Dec. 27, 1986).

42. *People's Daily* (Dec. 28, 1986), cited in *China Daily* (Dec. 29, 1986), p. 1.

43. These comments on Nanjing are based on discussions with foreign students at Nanjing University who visited Fudan.

44. Voice of America (Dec. 26, 1986).

45. *South China Morning Post* (Dec. 26, 1986). "Student-police clash in Tianjin," AFP (Dec. 25, 1986); FBIS (Dec. 29, 1986), p. R 6.

46. *Renmin Ribao* (Dec. 25, 1986). Cited in "Anarchism is not democracy," *China Daily* (Dec. 26, 1986), p. 4.

47. "Beijing issues new rules on public meetings," *China Daily* (Dec. 27, 1986), p. 1.

48. Lo Ping, "The Huangpu Jiang roars on."

49. Voice of America (Dec. 30, 1986).

50. Voice of America (Jan. 1, 1987). "Vigilance urged on the heels of 2 arrests," *China Daily* (Jan. 2, 1987), p. 3.

51. "Students demonstrate in Beijing," *China Daily* (Jan. 2, 1987), p. 1.

52. Voice of America (Jan. 2, 3, 1987).

53. Voice of America (Jan. 5, 1987).

54. Voice of America (Jan. 6, 1987).

55. Voice of America (Jan. 9, 1987). "African students march," *China Daily* (Jan. 9, 1987), p. 1. "Students' group raps 'false letter,'" *China Daily* (Jan. 9, 1987), p. 3.

56. "Officials talk with African students," *China Daily* (Jan. 10, 1987), p. 1.

57. Voice of America (Jan. 8, 1987).

58. "Frontier guards hit back at Viets," *China Daily* (Jan. 8, 1987).

59. Lo Ping, "The Huangpu Jiang roars on."

60. Ibid.

61. "Coping with effects of rural influx," *China Daily* (Jan. 23, 1987), p. 4.

62. Lo Ping, "The truth about the Hu Yaobang incident," *Zheng Ming*, no. 112 (Feb. 1, 1987), p. 6–10; FBIS (Jan. 29, 1987), p. K 4.

63. "Two arrested for roles in incident," *China Daily* (Dec. 27, 1986).

64. Voice of America (Dec. 31, 1986).

65. Lo Ping, "The truth about the Hu Yaobang incident."

66. Lo Ping, "The Huangpu Jiang roars on."

67. "How the student demo happened," *China Daily* (Dec. 25, 1986), p. 4.

68. "Ban on 'big-character' posters reaffirmed," *China Daily* (Dec. 31, 1986), p. 4.

# 5

## The Conservative Backlash

Throughout the fall, as the reform movement gathered strength and finally overflowed into the streets, debate continued at top political levels. According to Hong Kong analysts, the Sixth Plenary Session of the 12th Central Committee, meeting at the end of September 1986, was a scene of argument more fierce than any other of the Deng era. Reformers wanted the agenda to focus on the program for structural change and on personnel appointments to consolidate reform. Conservatives blocked this agenda and limited discussion to a document defining principles for building socialism. Deng spoke about opposing "bourgeois liberalization." Reformers were on the defensive, able only to try to narrow the definition of "bourgeois liberalization" and to stop publication of Deng's views.[1]

The Secretariat of the Central Committee met in late November 1986 against this backdrop of ideological and personal animosities. Deng and Zhao Ziyang were said to have felt that Hu Yaobang had pushed too hard on political reform, and had created his own faction of associates from the Communist Youth League in the central leadership.[2] Deng was uncomfortable with Hu's openness in leadership style and wanted the party leadership to retain more control over politics. Indeed, since 1983, Deng had been hearing complaints about Hu from other senior leaders.[3]

In addition to ideological issues, personnel questions were important. Hu wanted a large scale, rapid rejuvenation of the leadership. In a meeting in Sichuan in May 1986, he hinted at compulsory retirement of senior cadres over age 60 (other sources say 70). This would have forced out more than one-third of the membership of the Central Committee.[4]

At the November Secretariat meeting, Hu implied he would welcome Deng's resignation, so that Hu could succeed him as chairman of the Central Military Commission and the Central Advisory Commission. Deng and the other elderly rulers were angry. They wanted no forced resignations for Deng or for themselves. The meeting concluded that Hu should step down instead and that Zhao Ziyang should be the new head of the party.[5] The situation was somewhat reminiscent of Lin Biao's fall from power in 1971 after he attempted to become China's formal head of state.

Deng reportedly criticized Hu again at a meeting of the party's Central Military Commission, which Deng chaired, in December 1986, and urged Hu to resign. The meeting began on December 11, and was still in session on December 25, that is, throughout the period of the student demonstrations. It was the largest such meeting since late 1978; the earlier meeting had coincided with the consolidation of Deng's leadership and reform policies.[6] Despite the "suggestion" from Deng, Hu refused to step down.[7]

The student demonstrations of December became intertwined with this high-level personnel issue. The demonstrations began in a spontaneous manner, but once started, politicians from Beijing tried to manipulate them. In Shanghai, they urged slogans and tactics supporting and attacking specific national leaders. Police efforts to avoid violence may have reflected advice from some central leaders. Rumors circulated that Hu Qiaomu and other leaders visited Shanghai at these crucial moments, but who did what remains obscure.[8]

It might be recalled that in previous leadership struggles, mass movements have emerged. If not created by central leaders, they have been used by factions in the center to attack their rivals. For example, Mao Zedong and his allies created and used the Red Guards to attack Liu Shaoqi and his associates. Hua Guofeng and leftist allies used the Tiananmen demonstrations to displace Deng in 1976. Deng, in turn, used the Democracy Movement to displace Hua Guofeng and his leftist rivals.[9] In each case, the leader eventually had to suppress the social forces that he had unleashed and/or utilized.[10]

After the demonstration in December 1986, both reform and conservative elements tried to use the student demonstrations to their best possible advantage. Reformers argued that students were basically well disciplined and constructive. A prime example of this approach was the statement of He Dongchang, Vice Minister of the State Education Commission, on December 30, 1986. He said that student demonstrations were no cause for alarm. He estimated that only a little more than 1 percent of China's 2 million university students (i.e., a little more than 20,000, far less than other observers had estimated) were directly involved. Demonstrators were mostly first and second year students, who were "inevitably inexperienced." He considered it was "quite understandable" that students hoped to speed up present reforms.[11]

Conservatives criticized student demands for democracy and human rights. A *People's Daily* editorial on December 29 reminded readers of the four cardinal principles. It argued that China's socialist democracy required Communist Party leadership and the socialist system. Capitalist democracy was criticized as a form of bourgeois rule, serving capitalist private ownership. Running election campaigns in capitalist countries was not an opportunity for everybody because it was very costly. China already had a socialist democracy, shared by the overwhelming majority of the people and serving socialist public ownership. As for students, they should study hard, support the current nationwide reforms, and become well-disciplined people with high ideals and socialist ethics.[12]

## DENG ATTACKS THE STUDENTS AND HU YAOBANG

In the last few days of December 1986, Deng Xiaoping came down against the demonstrators, and simultaneously attacked Hu Yaobang again. Deng revealed his views in conversation with Chinese leaders on December 30. His comments were distributed confidentially throughout the Communist Party from January 2 to 7, 1987, as "CCP Central Directive No. 1." To the dismay of students and their allies, Deng was very negative:

It is not by any means permitted for [party and league members and all government and military personnel] to support the student disturbances in any way or form, or for them to take part in these disturbances. Those who violate this rule will be dealt with in accordance with the rules and regulations of the party, the communist youth league, and the education institutions concerned. Severe punishments will be meted out in cases where the circumstances are serious and in cases where those guilty of offenses fail to respond positively to re-education.[13]

When necessary, we must deal severely with those who defy orders. We can afford to shed some blood. Just try as much as possible not to kill anyone...

Look at Wei Jingsheng. We put him behind bars and the democracy movement died. We haven't released him but that didn't raise much of an international uproar...

These few years, we have been too lax in curbing the tides of bourgeois liberalism. Allowing some rightist influence is essential and correct, but we have gone overboard...

We cannot continue to make concessions in the face of current student troubles. We must remember this lesson (the current demonstrations) and increase our vigilance...[14]

In the circular, Deng singled out Fang Lizhi for criticism:

I have seen the statements made by Fang Lizhi. They are absolutely unlike what a party member ought to say. What point is there in allowing such a person to remain in the party? It is not a matter of persuading him to withdraw; he should be expelled.[15]

Deng also indicated explicit limitations on the democratization programs:

When we speak of democracy, we must not mean the implementation of capitalist democracy. We cannot set up such gimmicks as the division of powers between three branches of government. I always criticize the Americans and say that they really have three governments... This causes a great deal of trouble. This sort of device is not something our country can use.[16]

Deng commented favorably on the methods of the Polish leadership, and thus implied that martial law was not out of the question:

The leaders [of Poland] showed cool and level-headed judgment. Their attitude was firm. They were faced with a situation where the church and the labor unions were working in collusion with one another and were receiving support from the West. They resorted to military control to bring the situation under control. This proves that you cannot succeed without recourse to the methods of dictatorship. The methods of dictatorship should not only be talked about but should actually be employed when necessary.[17]

Deng also accused Hu Yaobang of doing nothing to stop the escalation of student demands.[18]

Deng was reportedly further angered when thousands of students demonstrated on January 1 at Tiananmen Square, contrary to specific orders. That was too close to home. Deng ordered that students be arrested, but Hu Yaobang temporized.[19] Deng also sent down directives with his harsh line.[20] This was quickly reflected in the official media. A *People's Daily* editorial on January 6 urged people to take a clear-cut stand against "bourgeois liberalization." (This was defined as the idea of negating the socialist system in favor of capitalism.) The editorial, reportedly penned by conservative ideologue Hu Qiaomu,[21] confidently said, "There is no ideological and material basis for turmoil in China, and the policies and lines worked out by the Party and government are correct and appreciated." Although the demonstrations were serious events, they were "the inevitable outcome of the weakness of some comrades in fighting the spread of bourgeois liberalization." It was charged that some people wanted to lead China's current policies in the direction of capitalism. "Some of our comrades have turned a blind eye to all this, but now it is time for them to wake up."[22] The clear and disturbing implication of this was that the student demonstrations were far more than simply misguided. Instead, they were now interpreted as part of an anti-socialist movement, fomented by class enemies.

Directive No. 1 had a direct impact on me, as a visiting professor interested in the student movement. Colleagues and students received the documents or heard briefings on the documents, and some students heard the directive also. Suddenly colleagues and students were less willing to discuss political issues with me. Warm relations chilled overnight. The text of the directive was not available to me at the time but the significance of the directive was obvious.

Within days, Prof. Fang Lizhi was purged (for the second time) from the Communist Party and from his administrative position also. He was attacked primarily for advocating "complete Westernization." He was reassigned to a research institute in Beijing, where his wife, a professor of physics at Beijing University, lived.[23] Thousands of his students reportedly sent him off at the train station, emotionally urging him to return.[24]

The president of his university, Prof. Guan Weiyuan, also was removed and reassigned to a research position.[25] Liu Binyan, the distinguished, muckraking writer associated with *People's Daily*, was also criticized and expelled from the party. His recent writings, it was said, falsely showed the degeneration of the party.[26] After his expulsion, fan mail poured into his editor's office.[27]

Wang Ruowang, a popular Shanghai writer and philosopher, who had supported the theory of humanism, was also expelled from the party.[28] Wang was quoted as having said at Tongji University, "I will defend bourgeois liberalization. That is what I want. If I am not given freedom, I will fight for it.... Capitalism is what present China needs, and needs urgently. We overstepped this stage and we can go back to make up for the missed stage."[29] Wang's house was searched, generating sympathy for him and disquiet among Shanghai intellectuals. This was too reminiscent of the cultural revolution.[30]

Both Fang and Wang had been singled out for criticism by Deng in Directive No. 1. Both Liu and Wang had suffered as rightists in the 1950s. In fall 1986 they had been professionally active, and important symbols of the party's treatment toward intellectuals.[31]

Peng Zhen, meeting with China's top policeman and other leaders (not including Hu Yaobang), stressed the importance of struggling against bourgeois liberalization and emphasized the need to support the four cardinal principles. These new struggles, he warned, were as important as the old struggle against spiritual pollution.[32]

Hu Yaobang could no longer resist the conservative tide. He dropped from public view after December 28. Hu reportedly spoke personally with Deng around January 2, and was told to resign.[33] He did.[34] Hu failed to meet a visiting Japanese politician because of a "cold," and was absent at important events. A spokesman for the foreign ministry refused to confirm that Hu was the general secretary of the party.[35]

A crucial, enlarged meeting of the Politbureau was held on January 6 (and perhaps continuing January 10–16), involving the Politbureau, members of the Central Advisory Commision, the Discipline Inspection Commission, the Central Secretariat, and others, all of whom were granted the right to vote despite provisions of the party constitution to the contrary.[36] Hu, Zhao Ziyang, and other top leaders offered self-criticisms. Zhao admitted that political errors had led to the student demonstrations, and that economic reforms were too hasty.[37] At the enlarged Politbureau meeting, Hu publicly resigned on January 16.[38] Premier Zhao Ziyang took over the party leadership position.

There was a certain irony and continuity in Hu Yaobang's fall. A decade earlier, after the Tiananmen demonstrations in April 1976, Deng Xiaoping had been blamed for fomenting disturbances and had been ousted from office. Now Deng, the former victim, used the same logic to remove his heir-apparent.

My students and colleagues seemed very surprised by the rapid downfall of Hu Yaobang. Whatever they knew of personal politics at the top levels, they did not share with me. It seemed as though Hu had grown in stature with his resignation. Before his resignation, he was considered a liberal and Westernizer, but not regarded with great esteem or affection. Overnight, he became the new symbol of reform.[39]

In the next weeks, more high level officials were dismissed. The president and vice president of the Chinese Academy of Sciences, Lu Jiaxi and Yan Dongsheng, were discharged on January 22. Lu Jiaxi was a leader in the Chinese Peasants and Workers Democratic Party, and a symbol of the new role of noncommunist intellectuals. The academy supervised Fang Lizhi's Chinese University of Science and Technology.[40] Party propaganda chief Zhu Houze was demoted to the position of deputy director of the Rural Development Center under the State Council.[41] The expulsion of the Agence Presse Francaise correspondent Lawrence MacDonald[42] and the arrest of a student on the very serious charge of spying for allegedly providing him information could only heighten fears. Moreover it was assumed the purge would expand. The Hong Kong press indicated that the writings of a hundred Chinese intellectuals might be restricted. Among the included scholars and professors were Su Shaozhi and Yan Jiaqi, whose insights on reform have been quoted extensively in this book.[43]

Further insight into Deng's views were distributed as the Central Committee's Document No. 2 around January 10.[44] *People's Daily* drew attention to Deng's speeches stressing the need to fight bourgeois liberalization, and to adhere to the four cardinal principles. Deng raised the classic image of chaos to get support for the communist party's leadership:

The unity of our people, the stability of society, the development of democracy, and the unification of our party hang on party leadership. This is an unshakeable principle. Otherwise, China will retrogress and be thrown into chaos. It will be impossible for us to realize modernization.[45]

The specific charges against Hu were outlined in the Central Committee's Document No. 3, issued on January 17, 1987.[46] Hu had erred by 1) not advocating rule by law, and by interfering with the independence of the judiciary; 2) opposing criticism of spiritual pollution and bourgeois liberalization; 3) being lenient toward Fang Lizhi; 4) advocating gross consumerism; and 5) inviting thousands of young Japanese to visit China. Some speculated Hu might eventually be made chairman of the Chinese People's Political Consultative Conference, as a face-saving gesture.[47]

The intensity of Deng's comments and the purges of Hu Yaobang, Fang Lizhi, and other high officials and liberal intellectuals left my associates confused. Some were pessimistic and distraught. They felt betrayed by Deng, whom they had trusted to guide China toward reform. They felt there was now no hope for reform. They worried that China was on the verge of an anti-reform, anti-right movement, perhaps reminiscent of the anti-spiritual pollution campaign of 1983, the cultural revolution of 1966–1976, or the anti-rightist campaign of 1956, following the "one hundred flowers" campaign. The parallels with this situation exactly thirty years earlier were disturbing, especially after Vice Premier Wan Li had assured them that the old history would not be repeated. Gloomy intellectuals even remembered the anti-reform campaign of 1898, when China's young emperor attempted reform. Conservatives in the court terminated the reform movement after 100 days; some reform leaders were executed and the xenophobic Boxer Rebellion followed. From a procedural point of view, it seemed that China was returning to the era in which one leader's whims shaped the destiny of the whole nation.

A few people thought that reform would continue. They realized that structural reform would be a gradual process over many years, and that it could succeed only in a stable political environment. Some argued that the reform program was not dependent on Hu Yaobang and could survive his fall. If they knew about the personal politics of top leaders and how this contributed to Hu's departure, they did not say anything to me about it.

No liberal intellectual in China, from high to low level, dared to offer a public reply. A remarkable reaction did, however, come from Chinese students in the United States on January 19, 1987. They sent a public statement to the communist party's Central Committee and the State Council, expressing concern about the dismissals of Hu Yaobang, Fang Lizhi, Liu Binyan, Wang Ruowang, and others. About 949 students endorsed the statement, and half of them courageously signed publicly.[48]

Top leaders tried to reassure intellectuals that reforms would continue. On January 13, Deng Xiaoping commented that China would continue reform in an orderly way. He stressed that without political stability and unity, it would be impossible for China to continue its economic construction and the opening up of policy and reform.[49]

Chen Junsheng, secretary general of the State Council, said that China would continue its established policies of reform and opening to the outside world. Reform is a complicated process, which calls for substantial effort, he noted. Democracy, he said, is also a long-term process. Without democracy, there would be no socialism or socialist modernization. But democracy and modernization should progress step by step.[50]

Li Xiannian, head of state, assured that China's policy of opening to the outside world was a set policy and would not change.[51] Premier and new acting party head Zhao Ziyang commented tht there had been no changes in China's original plans for financial reform and other managerial changes.[52] Vice Premier Li Peng tried to assure intellectuals that there would be no change in policy toward them, and that they were not the target of the new anti-bourgeois liberalization campaign.[53] Vice Premier Tian Jiyun, in Japan, stressed that China's policy was to continue with its openness policy and to carry out overall reforms.[54] Deng further reiterated the open door policy. "If there are any shortcomings in implementing our open policy, the main one is that China needs further opening."[55]

Zhao Ziyang again emphasized that China would not launch any political campaign that would, in any sense, smack of the chaos of the late 1960s and the early 1970s.[56] He then told a large meeting celebrating the spring festival:

The current work of opposing bourgeois liberalization will be strictly limited to the Chinese Communist Party, and conducted mainly in the political ideological field. It will not be conducted in rural areas. And in enterprises and institutions only positive education will be carried out. . . . No 'leftist' mistakes will be repeated, or will be permitted.[57]

Zhao also implied that the program of political reform would continue:

We have listed a high degree of democracy as one of the unshakeable targets for building a socialist country. . . . election methods at the county level will be further improved, including nominating more candidates for election than required for each post.[58]

A *People's Daily* editorial further specified the limits of the new movement:

... the current campaign against bourgeois liberalization is strictly limited to the party and ideological aspects ... The campaign should not affect the economic reform, rural policy, scientific and technological research, exploration of new literary and artistic styles and techniques or people's life. Rural areas, democratic parties and non-communist intellectuals will not be involved.[59]

These and other documents specifying how to handle anti-bourgeois liberalization activities were distributed around January 28 as Central Committee Document No. 4.[60]

Vice Premier Li Peng staked out a more conservative stand against the students in February. He charged that the December student demonstrations "resulted from years of vague and wavering attitudes toward the trend of bourgeois liberalization," and "they were wrong and had bad social effects, no matter what motives the students had." Li said that careful and thorough investigations into the attitudes of college students were necessary: "Only by paying close attention to the ideas and thoughts of college students can we achieve good results in ideological work." Li also called for the establishment of suitable channels through which students could express opinions and suggestions:

We should take into consideration reasonable suggestions and demands from students and improve our work earnestly ... We should give patient and clear explanations to those suggestions that, though reasonable, cannot be put into effect quickly, and for unreasonable demands, instead of making facile promises, we should give clear reasons why we oppose them.[61]

Even conservative octogenarian Peng Zhen promised continuation of some reforms. A speech he gave in October 1986 was distributed in January 1987. Peng argued China could continue to learn some industrial management techniques. However, he stressed that China had to retain a socialist and Marxist approach. Democratization had to be within the framework of party leadership and the principle of democratic dictatorship.[62] In later comments, he rejected the concept of pluralism and of different political interests. He recognized, however, that some administrative changes could continue to be made in economic management.[63] Chinese theorists now dismissed pluralism: "In China there is no social foundation for complicated factional struggles as in the capitalist world, because the fundamental interests of Chinese workers, farmers, and intellectuals are identical."[64]

A theoretical article in *People's Daily* confirmed opposition to political reform. The author put democratic reforms off into the vague, distant future: "... democratic life can only be further developed when the level of productive forces has been enhanced to a higher level." A higher level of economy was needed so people would have leisure time and cultural, scientific, and administrative ability. China needed an orderly, gradual advance, that "is not a struggle which mainly relies on the spontaneous activities and support of the masses.... Using a legal system and discipline to dispel unrest, and using people's democratic dictatorship to overcome chaos is an indispensible measure..."[65]

Zhao Ziyang walked a very narrow line at the Fifth Session of the 6th National People's Congress in March 1987. On the one hand, he said that bourgeois liberalization had been curbed. Nevertheless, immense efforts must be made to eliminate the pernicious influence of this erroneous ideological trend. On the other hand, he argued that under no circumstances is it permissible to stifle democracy on the pretext of opposing bourgeois liberalism, or to resist and even crack down upon the justified criticism of errors and mistakes in party work. He insisted that economic reforms and an open policy would continue.[66]

## THE FUTURE OF REFORM

Will China's reforms continue? Will youth resume demonstrating? Will they be won over by the party's arguments that they were young, naive, unsophisticated, and unhistorical about politics, or will they simply become more alienated? Will the conservative faction be able to reverse the reforms? Will the reform faction take back the initiative?

These questions are intertwined with personnel questions. Will Deng retire from office before he dies? Who will replace Zhao Ziyang as premier?[67] A reformer, a conservative, or an unknown who is accepted by all factions? Will Zhao Ziyang stay head of the party?

Certainly, discussion of reform is now in a new environment. But that does not mean that all reforms will be halted. Top leaders continued to endorse economic reform. One writer struggled to distinguish economic reforms from bourgeois liberalization:

The reform measures currently in practice ... were aimed at breaking the old economic pattern that binds the development of productivity and perfecting the socialist system rather than negating such a system, as the advocates of "total Westernization" would do.

[T]he director responsibility system for the enterprise was not intended to weaken or eliminate the party's leadership, but to separate such leadership from management, so that the party organizations could better concentrate on the ideological and moral cultivation of employees. The leasing of enterprises to collectives and individuals was adopted to separate ownership and management so as to enliven the enterprises. The issuing of stock shares and the auction of a few smaller enterprises to individuals was aimed at diversifying the economy with public ownership as the backbone. The reform of the distribution system was intended to break the "big pot" system and pay people according to their work rather than to widen the gap between the rich and the poor as under the capitalist system. Enterprises in hopeless financial positions were declared bankrupt to solve the problem that enterprises were not responsible for their losses.

All in all, these measures indicated that we were borrowing critically, rather than imitating indiscriminately, the experience of Western countries in management and adapting it to Chinese conditions. ... The reform measures should be carried on firmly as long as they meet our actual needs ... [68]

The objective need for other reforms remains. Five months after the fall of Hu Yaobang, as the Communist Party of China was preparing for its critical Thirteenth Party Congress in October 1987, Deng clearly endorsed the basic concepts of reform. Using a meeting with a high Yugoslavian official as an opportunity to comment on reform, he said:

China is now carrying out a reform. I am all in favor of that. There is no other solution for us. After years of practice, it turned out that the old stuff didn't work ... So in 1978, ... we drew up a series of new principles and policies, the major ones being reform and the open policy.

Although endorsing reform in principle, Deng was vague about political reform:

Now a new question has been raised, reform of the political structure. This will be one of the main topics at the Thirteenth National Party Congress to be held next October. It's a complicated issue. ... Generally speaking, reform of the political structure involves democratization, but what that means is not very clear.[69]

There are important constraints on the conservative faction that will limit the extent of the backlash in the short term. First, many of the economic and cultural reforms are very popular. The availability of consumer goods (color television, refrigerators, stereo systems, etc.), the expansion of housing, the improvement of clothing, the access to Western classical and popular music on radio and tape, the encouragement of fun (symbolized by disco dancing and the reconversion of Shanghai's Great World back to an entertainment center from a Children's Palace)—these types of policies are all very popular. The conservatives did criticize Hu Yaobang for a consumption-led economic policy. If they try to reverse this, they will find that austerity will be very unpopular.

Second, economic growth is needed to provide the material foundation for such improvements. This will require continued reforms in the economic system to improve efficiency. This includes reforms in management, employment, and the ownership system. Improvement in technology will still be needed to enable China to expand exports. These factors mean that at a minimum, some continued economic reform is irrevocable.

Third, foreign investment is needed to provide continued access to capital, technology, and markets. While international business does not require democracy and typically is comfortable in an authoritarian environment, it does seek stability to facilitate long-term planning. The conservative faction will be constrained by the need to assure a stable business environment. The foreign business community was reported to be alarmed by the anti-bourgeois liberalization campaign, with its overtones of anti-Westernism and its reminder of China's history of policy shifts.[70] Hu Yaobang had successfully throttled the anti-spiritual pollution campaign in 1983 on this basis.[71]

A fourth constraint involves Hong Kong and Taiwan. A vigorous campaign against reform and bourgeois liberalization will cause a deep reaction in Hong Kong, and could undermine plans for graceful absorption after 1997. This in turn would give people in Taiwan new reasons for fearing reunification with the mainland.

In general the international environment is very different from in the past. In the 1950s, when the hundred flowers campaign turned into the anti-rightist movement, the United States was hostile, and there were no obvious incentives for reform. In the 1980s, the international political and economic environment supports domestic reform, and will extract a price if China reverses the reforms it has undertaken already.

Another reason to think the backlash will not be too strong is the likelihood that it reflected personality and personnel issues that will pass with time. Conservative senior leaders did not want Hu Yaobang to be Deng's successor. It was important to have him removed before Deng died or retired. They finally prevailed on Deng. Moreover, some top leaders may have reacted against the anti-corruption campaigns in early 1986 that had punished (and sometimes executed) their children. Two China watchers warned, "In scapegoating sons of certain hardliners and military leaders, reformers risk aggravating dormant enmities and creating precisely the kind of factional struggle and disunity they hope to avoid."[72] One observer suggested that revenge was directed at Hu Yaobang because he had called for punishment of Peng Zhen's daughter and Hu Qiaomu's son for economic crimes.[73] Conservatives may have been eagerly seeking a new political campaign to deflect the old one and to put their attackers on the defensive. The same analyst and others believed that key military leaders opposed Hu Yaobang.[74] Finally, some senior leaders did not want to be forced into retirement. Indeed, after the fall of Hu Yaobang, there were signs that senior cadres might not be forced to resign. "Waves that come after will not overtake the waves that come first," aged President Li Xiannian was quoted as saying.[75]

For these reasons it is unlikely that the campaign against bourgeois liberalization will be very deep and vigorous. Indeed, the leadership has indicated that the movement will be limited to party members only, not to everyone. In May 1987, one of those arrested in December for inciting riot was given a three year jail sentence. Compared with the 10 and 15 year sentences for participants in the Democracy Movement in 1980, this was a relatively light sentence.

At the same time, the backlash proved that senior party and military leaders will control the depth and pace of reform. The crucial decisions about reform remain to be made in the future. Perhaps by the end of 1987, policy will be clearer. However, China is entering an interregnum and a succession period. Several years may be needed for the new leadership to emerge and to consolidate power. Only then will the complex issue of political reform be tackled again.

In this regard, it is well to recall Deng Xiaoping's personal history. He was dismissed from high office during the cultural revolution and again in 1976, when he was blamed for the Tiananmen demonstrations. He came back to high office both times. Indeed, in the process of coming back, he gained personal support for the reform program. Will his close follower Hu Yaobang, also blamed for mass demonstrations, attempt the same type of political comeback? It is premature to consider Hu Yaobang permanently out of the leadership.[76]

In the struggle for and against reform, the electoral process will probably not be very important. Direct elections for people's congresses at county and township levels were carried out in spring 1987, in the wake of the conservative backlash.[77] Under such circumstances, no one could openly challenge the conservative trend. Some steps were taken in the election process to avoid confrontation. In Tianjin, local officials withdrew their initial nominations and did allow for more nominations, thereby opening up the process.[78] Local elections were held there in mid-January.[79] Care was taken to ensure that there would be more candidates than positions. There were some complaints about illegal practices that deprived voters of real choices, and some people had no understanding of the election process.

In general, the student movement made no effort to play a role in the local elections.[80] Student activists were younger and less experienced in 1987 than were the activists of 1980, who had been sent down to the countryside after high school.[81]

In Beijing University's election district, however, the student movement made a mark in elections in late May. Prof. Fang Lizhi received many write-in votes for a seat as delegate to the National People's Congress. Government officials nullified his votes, claiming him ineligible because he had run in Anhui, before his dismissal from his academic post there.[82] Fang Lizhi's wife, Prof. Li Shuxian, a physicist at Beijing University, was elected representative to the local people's congress. About 90 percent of students voted.[83]

The Thirteenth Party Congress, scheduled for October 1987, will be a crucial milestone marking the next stage of China's politics.[84] However the issue of reform will take more time. Deng gave a realistic (and perhaps optimistic) prediction of the time-frame for reform:

It took three years for the rural economic reform to achieve good results, and it should take from three to five years for the urban economic reform to produce the visible results we expect. Reform of the political structure will be more complicated. In certain aspects, results can be obtained in from three to five years, but in certain others it may take ten.[85]

Hungary, it was pointed out, had been carrying out reforms for twenty years, and was still making new reforms.[86]

## NOTES

1. Lo Ping, "Deng Xiaoping criticizes Chen Yun at meeting," *Zheng Ming*, no. 108 (Oct. 1, 1986), pp. 8–12; FBIS (Oct. 9, 1986), pp. 1–10. Lo Ping, "Note on a northern journey—reformists suffer setback for the first time," *Zheng Ming*, no. 109 (Nov. 1, 1986), pp. 6–10; FBIS (Nov. 18, 1986), pp. K 1–9. Deng Xiaoping, "Remarks at the 6th Plenary Session of the party's 12th Central Committee," Sept. 28, 1986, *Beijing Review*, no. 26 (June 29, 1987), p. 14.

2. KYODO (Jan. 17, 1987); Hong Kong AFP (Jan. 19, 1987); FBIS (Jan. 20, 1987), pp. K 3–6.

3. Kuang Pi-hua, "Questions concerning who will replace Zhao, and the mystery of Hua's resignation," *Hong Kong Kuang Chiao Ching*, no. 173 (Feb. 16, 1987), pp. 6–9; FBIS (Feb. 20, 1987), p. K 8.

4. "Rejuvenation called 'key reason' for Hu's downfall," *Hong Kong Standard* (Feb. 6, 1987), p. 8; FBIS (Feb. 9, 1987), pp. K 2–3.

5. Lo Ping, "The truth about the Hu Yaobang incident," *Zheng Ming*, no. 112 (Feb. 1, 1987), pp. 6–10; FBIS (Jan. 29, 1987), p. K 2.

6. "Central military commission meets," *China Daily* (Dec. 26, 1986), p. 1.

7. "Deng urges Hu Yaobang to resign, Hu refuses," *KYODO* (Jan. 14, 1987); FBIS (Jan. 14, 1987), p. K 1.

8. Lo Ping, "The Huangpu Jiang roars on," *Zheng Ming*, no. 111 (Jan. 1, 1987); FBIS (Jan. 8, 1987), p. K 5.

9. Stanley Rosen, "Guangzhou's democracy movement in cultural revolution perspective," *China Quarterly*, no. 101 (March 1985), pp. 1–31.

10. Edward Friedman, "The societal obstacle to China's socialist transition: state capitalism or feudal fascism," in Victor Nee and David Mozingo (eds.), *State and Society in Contemporary China* (Ithaca, NY: Cornell University Press, 1983), pp. 148–71.

11. "Students' demos are 'no cause for alarm,'" *China Daily* (Dec. 31, 1986).

12. "Why socialist road is the only course," *China Daily* (Dec. 30, 1986), p. 4.

13. *Inside China Mainland* (April 1987), p. 1. An edited version appeared as "Take a clear-cut stand against bourgeois liberalization," *Beijing Review*, no. 26 (June 29, 1987), p. 15–16. See also, "Internal papers show Deng position on crackdown," AFP (Feb. 26, 1987); FBIS (Feb. 26, 1987), pp. K 1–2. Lo Ping, "The drive to overthrow Hu has intensified to a major crisis," *Zheng Ming*, no. 113 (March 1, 1987), pp. 6–10; FBIS (March 3, 1987), pp. K 1–8.

14. Lulu Yu, "Deng orders party crackdown on liberals," *South China Morning Post* (Jan. 12, 1987), p. 1.

15. *Inside China Mainland* (April 1987), p. 2.

16. Ibid.

17. Ibid.

18. "Deng urges Hu Yaobang to resign, Hu refuses."

19. Chuang Ming, "Zhao Ziyang receives instruction in time of danger to save a desparate situation," *Hong Kong Ching Pao* (Feb. 10, 1987), pp. 27–29; FBIS (Feb. 12, 1987), p. K 5.

20. Lo Ping, "The truth about the Hu Yaobang incident."

21. Pai Yen, "Drastic actions taken by Hu Qiaomu and Deng Liqun to oppose bourgeois liberalizations," *Zheng Ming*, no. 113 (March 1, 1987), pp. 16–18; FBIS (March 5, 1987), p. K 12.

22. "Paper raps capitalist tendency," *China Daily* (Jan. 7, 1987), p. 1.

23. "'Complete Westernization' negates socialism," *Beijing Review*, no. 3 (Jan. 19, 1987), p. 16.

24. Marlowe Hood, "Anti-liberalization drive reportedly opposed," *South China Morning Post* (Feb. 23, 1987), p. 8; FBIS (Feb. 24, 1987), p. K 6.

25. "University leaders in Hefei replaced," *China Daily* (Jan. 13, 1987), p. 1.

26. "Newspaper reporter expelled from party," *China Daily* (Jan. 26, 1987), p. 1.

27. Marlowe Hood, "Anti-liberalization drive reportedly opposed."

28. "Shanghai writer is expelled from Party," *China Daily* (Jan. 15, 1987), p. 1.

29. NCNA (Jan. 18, 1987); FBIS (Jan. 21, 1987), p. K 21.

30. Chang Chie-feng, "Document no. 2 to 6 reveal current situation," *Hong Kong Pai Hsing*, no. 138 (Feb. 16, 1987); FBIS (Feb. 17, 1987), p. K 15.

31. Fang Bin, "Wang Ruoshui case not yet settled," *Ching Pao*, no. 9 (Sept. 10, 1986); FBIS (Sept. 24, 1986), p. K 1.

32. "Peng Zhen opposes bourgeois liberalization," *NCNA* (Jan. 12, 1987); FBIS (Jan. 12, 1987), p. K 4.

33. Lo Ping, "The drive to overthrow Hu has intensified to a major crisis."

34. Pai Yen, "Drastic actions taken by Hu Qiaomu and Deng Liqun to oppose bourgeois liberalization."

35. "Hu replacement questioned," *KYODO* (Jan. 12, 1987); FBIS (Jan. 12, 1987), p. K 3. "No comment on replacement," *TANJUG* (Jan. 12, 1987); FBIS (Jan. 12, 1987), p. K 5.

36. Lo Ping, "The drive to overthrow Hu has intensified to a major crisis."

37. "Zhao makes self-criticism for political mistakes," *KYODO* (Jan. 25, 1987); FBIS (Jan. 27, 1987), p. K 8.

38. "Hu Yaobang resigns as General Secretary," *NCNA* (Jan. 16, 1987); FBIS (Jan. 16, 1987), p. K 1. "Hu Yaobang resigns from top job," *China Daily* (Jan. 17, 1987), p. 1.

39. Hong Kong AFP (Jan. 17, 1987). "Cool Response to Hu Yaobang's fall, Shanghai student unrest will not erupt again," Hong Kong AFP (Jan. 19, 1987); FBIS (Jan. 20, 1987), pp. K 12–14.

40. "Academy head named," *China Daily* (Jan. 23, 1986), p. 1.

41. "New party department chief named," *China Daily* (Feb. 5, 1987), p. 1.

42. "AFP reporter asked to leave," *China Daily* (Jan. 27, 1987), p. 1.

43. Huang Yanglie, "China resolutely opposes liberal trends of thought, one hundred people will be restricted in expressing their views," *Ming Pao* (Jan. 23, 1987), p. 2; FBIS (Jan. 23, 1987), p. K 10. Su Shaozhi has left the party.

44. Kuang Pi-hua, "Questions concerning who will replace Zhao, and the mystery of Hu's resignation," *Hong Kong Kuang Chiao Ching*, no. 173 (Feb. 16, 1987), pp. 6–9; FBIS (Feb. 20, 1987), p. K 6.

45. Su Ji, "Powerful weapon for opposing bourgeois liberalization—restudying the 'Selected Works of Deng Xiaoping,'" *People's Daily* (Jan. 19, 1987); FBIS (Jan. 20, 1987), p. K 1; FBIS (Jan. 21, 1987), pp. K 5–8.

46. "What happened to Hu Yaobang," *Inside China Mainland* (May 1987), pp. 1–3.

47. Huang Yang-lieh, "Hu Yaobang will succeed Li Xiannian as President of the PRC; Central Committee issues documents on Hu's mistakes," *Ming Pao* (Jan. 26, 1987), p. 2; FBIS (Jan. 27, 1987), p. K 5. Lu Tzu-chien, "Hu Yaobang's five mistakes," *Ming Pao* (Jan. 31, 1987), p. 2; FBIS (Feb. 2, 1987), p. K 1. Chang Chieh-feng, "Document No. 1 to 6 reveal current situation," *Hong Kong Pai Hsing*, no. 138 (Feb. 16, 1987); FBIS (Feb. 17, 1987), p. K 15. *KYODO* (March 7, 1987); FBIS (March 9, 1987), p. K 1.

48. *China Spring*, no. 45 (March 1987), pp. 50–53.

49. "China vows to persist in open policy and reform," *China Daily* (Jan. 14, 1987), p. 1.

50. "Socialism: correct choice for China," *China Daily* (Jan. 14, 1987), p. 4.

51. "State firm in its open policy—Li," *China Daily* (Jan. 16, 1987).

52. "China reaffirms open policy," *China Daily* (Jan. 20, 1987), p. 1.

53. "Intellectuals are not the target—Li Peng," *China Daily* (Jan. 19, 1987), p. 1.

54. "China reaffirms open policy."

55. "Reality is the base of policy, Deng," *China Daily* (Jan. 21, 1987), p. 1.

56. "Policy will continue," *China Daily* (Jan. 26, 1987), p. 4.

57. "Zhao rules out political campaign over 'liberalization,'" *China Daily* (Jan. 30, 1987), p. 1.

58. "Zhao promises democratic steps," *China Daily* (Jan. 31, 1987), p. 1.

59. "Combating limited to party," *China Daily* (Feb. 4, 1987).

60. Chang Chieh-feng, "Document no. 2 to 6 reveal current situation."

61. "Li urges colleges to arrange more outside experiences," *China Daily* (Feb. 17, 1987), p. 1.

62. Speech on Oct. 28, 1986, reprinted in *Red Flag*, no. 2 (1987), and *People's Daily Overseas Edition* (Jan. 15, 1987), p. 5; FBIS (Jan. 16, 1987), p. K 6.

63. "Peng Zhen answers journalists' questions," *Beijing Review*, no. 17 (April 27, 1987), pp. 14–15.

64. "The 'conservative'/'reformist' myth," *Beijing Review*, no. 17 (April 27, 1987), p. 5.

65. Li Jiapeng, "Building of democracy as viewed from the overall scheme of modernization," *People's Daily* (Feb. 23, 1987), p. 5; FBIS (Feb. 27, 1987), pp. K 2–5.

66. Zhao Ziyang, "Report on the work of government," *Beijing Review*, no. 16 (April 20, 1987), pp. xvi–xvii.

67. Speculation focused on Wan Li, Li Peng, Qiao Shi, and Tian Jiyun. *Ming Pao* (Jan. 21, 1987), p. 2; FBIS (Jan. 21, 1987).

68. *Bright Daily*, cited in "Reform must be continued," *China Daily* (Feb. 16, 1987), p. 4.

69. "Deng calls for speedup in reform," *Beijing Review*, no. 34 (Aug. 24, 1987), pp. 13, 15.

70. Marlowe Hood, "Serious alarm among foreign business community," *South China Morning Post* (Feb. 26, 1987), p. 8; FBIS (Feb. 26, 1987), p. K 22.

71. Lo Bing, "The drive to overthrow Hu Yaobang has intensified to a major crisis," *Zheng Ming*, no. 113 (March 1, 1987), p. 6–10; FBIS (March 3, 1987), p. K 5.

72. Liang Heng and Judith Shapiro, "In China, the year—and claws—of the tiger," *New York Times* (March 8, 1986), Section I, p. 27.

73. Rumors about shady business deals of Peng Zhen's children are reported in "Peng Zhen's daughter denies corruption rumor," *Hong Kong Standard* (Oct. 12, 1986), p. 6; FBIS (Oct. 15, 1986), p. K 24.

74. Wang Bingzhang, "Cause and consequence," *China Spring Digest*, (March/April, 1987), p. 40.

75. David Wong, *Hong Kong Standard* (March 9, 1987), p. 8; FBIS (March 11, 1987), p. K 6.

76. Lo Bing, "The drive to overthrow Hu has intensified to a major crisis."

77. "Do a good job of electing county and township people's deputies," *People's Daily* (Jan. 14, 1987); FBIS (Feb. 3, 1987), p. K 3.

78. *South China Morning Post* (Dec. 16, 1986).

79. "Tianjin elects local deputies," *China Daily* (Jan. 20, 1987), p. 3.

80. Li Ning and Wu Naitao, "The election process in Tianjin," *Beijing Review*, no. 13 (March 30, 1987), pp. 22–23.

81. Chuang Ming, "Zhao Ziyang receives instructions in time of danger to save a desperate situation," *Hong Kong Ching Pao* (Feb. 10, 1987), pp. 18–29; FBIS (Feb. 12, 1987), p. K 4.

82. Marlowe Hood, "Fang had many write-in votes," *South China Morning Post* (May 29, 1987), p. 1; FBIS (May 29, 1987), pp. K 4–5.

83. "Fang Lizhi's wife elected district people's deputy," *Hong Kong Zhongguo Tongxun she* (May 29, 1987); FBIS (May 29, 1987), p. K 3.

84. Yao Shing-mu and Chan Wai-fong, "Conservatives prepare for party congress," *Hong Kong Standard* (March 4, 1987), p. 8; FBIS (March 4, 1987), pp. K 1–3.

85. "Deng calls for speedup in reform," *Beijing Review*, no. 34 (Aug. 24, 1987), p. 16. See also "Beijing newspaper discloses the speech of an important CPC

official on the three targets for China's political reform," *Ta Kong Pao* (March 11, 1987); FBIS (March 11, 1987), p. K 8.

86. "Red Flag carries article suggesting that reform must not be carried out with undue haste," *NCNA* (March 15, 1987); FBIS (March 16, 1987), p. K 13.

# 6
# Conclusion

China is at a historical crossroads. It must choose between blazing a new trail toward an as-yet undefined, radically reformed socialism, or attempting moderate adjustments in its traditional socialist system. If it fails to do either, it will stagnate dangerously. All choices have their drawbacks, so conflict is inevitable.

The conservative backlash of 1987 has blocked radical reform for several years, but the radical reformers have had a partial victory. The idea of reform is now well established in Chinese politics. Even the conservatives now accept and trumpet the need for reform. The question is no longer whether China will reform, but rather how quickly, and in what way. China will not stagnate into a Soviet-style abyss. It is reforming in a cautious, step-by-step manner. How far this process will go over the coming decades cannot be known at this time. Cycles of authoritarian and liberal phases are likely to continue, but the authoritarian periods are likely to be progressively less strict, and the liberal phases are likely to be increasingly more free and open.

## CHINA'S POLITICAL DILEMMA

The events of 1986/87 both follow an old pattern and reveal a new one. In one way, the events followed an old script. Factional struggle breaks out some time prior to a major party congress. One faction mobilizes and uses mass support as a weapon. Another faction blames the first for risking chaos. The process resembles, in outward appearance, expanding democracy but ultimately, senior military leaders are the crucial arbiters. When leadership is consolidated again, these proto-democratic tendencies are terminated, and authoritarian rule is revived. In this regard, 1986/87 was like 1979–1981, 1976, 1966–1969, and 1956/57.

At the same time, the events of 1986/87 illuminate long-term changes in China that point toward a deep political dilemma. China's political system does not mesh well with economic and social needs. Therefore its legitimacy is fragile. This is due both to an unavoidable aging process of the Chinese revolution and to specific policy mistakes.

In China's political system, ultimate political power has been exercised by a group of about twenty people in their seventies and eighties. Their power comes from their positions in the Communist Party and the People's Liberation Army over the past five decades. They receive political input from various elements of society, but ultimately the strongest inputs come from their political associates in the party and state structure. The few hundred members of the party Central Committee and provincial leaders also have influence. Their approval must be obtained for major decisions.

On policy issues, the elite has been influenced by professionals in the specific fields, demonstrations, strikes, and other disturbances. Both Marxist-Leninist-Maoist concepts of mass line and Confucian principles of statecraft have demanded that they anticipate problems and act on them before they become serious. With regard to issues of personnel and power, however, this elite has been reluctant to share political power. The desire to retain power also resonates with both Marxist-Leninist and many traditional Confucian values. Leaders have felt threatened by proposals for radical political reform, and blocked them.

These elderly leaders may not be fully in touch with the way China has changed over the past four decades. Forty years ago, when the communist party led China's revolution, China had suffered a century of chaos, civil war, and international aggression. It had an intensive agricultural economy, with low output per capita. It needed a government that could impose order and unity, accelerate economic growth, and create an industrial base. The party, with its rural guerrilla army, was able to unify the country and start it on the road to reconstruction.

Today China is a reasonably powerful member of a complex interdependent global system. The world is characterized by rapid technological change, and China must keep up to be competitive. China's economy is large, with far more enterprises than can be administered centrally. Many enterprises have modern technology. Maintaining economic growth and transformation is a great challenge in the face of population pressures, resource limitations, and ecological constraints. Sophisticated management and appropriate incentives, not forced investment, are needed. In an era of internationalization of the factors of production and cultural values, defining and creating a modern "Chinese way" is especially difficult. The assets the Communist Party needed to win the revolution are not so relevant for today's new needs.

China's leadership is changing just as much as its problems are. The heroes who made the communist revolution have died. Today's senior leaders grew up in a world of class and international struggle. Many were from poor, rural backgrounds. They had no formal education or experience with the broader world. Their strength was their ability to mobilize masses for revolutionary changes. They too are rapidly passing from the scene. In a few years, all the active political leaders and even the semi-retired senior leaders will have matured in and served their full careers in China's socialist system. The problems they have faced were the problems created by their own socialist system, such as the cultural revolution. Their challenge is in economic development to modernize China's economy, not to further class struggle.

As the old generation of military heroes dies, the deep personal relationships between military and party will disappear. The newly emerging military-party relations, not tempered by battle, are presumably weaker. Will strong, institutionalized linkages be established? If not, new problems could emerge in maintaining civilian control over the military.

The new, emerging leadership is diverse and different. Some younger leaders are as parochial and selfish as their predecessors, or more so. They are using family connections to become the new generation of businessmen or politicians.

On the other hand, many new leaders from China's Red Guard generation are quite liberal. They know too well from personal experience the tragedies of unrestrained power, and also know the depths of China's economic and social problems. Some are seriously committed to economic and political reform. In some cases, they are children of high-ranking cadres, have excelled in studies at Beijing University, and have studied abroad. Such sophisticated people are the spearhead of the reform movement.[1]

China's population is different now also. The majority of people have grown up under the leadership of the Communist Party. For them, the party is not the revolutionary savior from feudal chaos. It is the party of the ruling establishment. The party can claim credit for accomplishments in the past decades, but it cannot escape responsibility for the problems China has faced in this period. Ineffective government policies and corruption are no longer associated with the pre-revolutionary government. They are blamed on the communist government. People are now living in the television era, and have images of the whole world in their homes. They compare their economic and political conditions with those of other countries in the world. Given all these changes, continuing old political strategies and symbols are highly problematical.

The generational shift in both leadership and masses is one crucial element in China's struggle over political reform. At its simplest level, the struggle is between young and old. Richard and Margaret Braungart provide the general theoretical framework in which to understand China's generational conflicts:

When society changes rapidly and the various cohorts come of age under divergent conditions, they are likely to develop different sets of political attitudes, thereby increasing the likelihood of generational conflict over politics ... [2]

This generational conflict is aggravated by the strong tendency in China's bureaucratic, Confucian system for age to be highly correlated with status and political and economic power. Old people are powerful. Thus generational conflict has an element of class conflict.

These profound changes over the past decades have contributed to a quiet but serious crisis of political legitimacy. Youth have been born into a pre-established political environment, and have had no opportunity to make a positive choice about politics. They are uncomfortable with their arranged political marriage. The widespread student demonstrations of December 1986 symbolized this. Dismissals of some popular intellectuals, attacks on bourgeois liberalization, and the fear of repression have silenced youth for a while, but have further eroded legitimacy. Of course this decline in legitimacy did not happen suddenly. It has been a gradual process, starting for most people at the end of the cultural revolution in the late 1960s.

Precisely the same transformation of youth in the Soviet Union has been observed by a Soviet emigré sociologist:

Youth in the Soviet Union have come to represent a social force that is gradually eroding the fundamentals of the system. Supporting the values of individualism, hedonism, and permissiveness, young people are the principal channel for the penetration of Western ideas, consumer goods, and music into Soviet society. [3]

Another source of the legitimacy problem for the central leadership lies in the weakness of institutional procedures. The central political system does not have a widely accepted, institutional mechanism to reach a clear, binding agreement on the complex policy choices dealing with reform. Debate continues indefinitely on reform. Certainly the procedures used to force Hu Yaobang's resignation lacked a sound base.

This issue of institutional legitimacy is especially important because the future generations of leaders lack the personal status to be strong leaders. Mao Zedong and Deng Xiaoping had personal charisma throughout the Chinese leadership and especially in the military, which evolved from decades of revolutionary struggle. They could enforce political decisions.

The next generation of leaders lacks this status. They are maturing in the far less glamorous minefields of bureaucratic politics, not in the battlefields of revolution. Why should some top leaders accept decisions by any other leader? Looking a few years back, they did not accept Hua Guofeng's power, partly because it lacked institutional legitimacy. Mao's anointment was not enough. Hu Yaobang's sudden collapse also showed the lack of institutionalized power, as well as the cleavage between the elderly party and military conservatives on the one hand and the young reformers on the other.

Under present conditions, China's next leaders can have only a weak institutionalized claim to legitimate power. Whoever is the next leader has no assurance that he will have support to stay in power or to implement any particular policies. His power will come from support of the elderly rulers and some factional coalition that will be somewhat unstable.

Succession in communist states has rarely worked out the way old leaders want. The top leader is reluctant to give his anointed successor enough power to consolidate his position. This stems from his own psychological inability to step down, as well as from opposition of rivals who fear early consolidation of power of the protégé. This heir-apparent's efforts to formalize his position fuel rivalries with others in the leadership group. The apparent successor eventually falters. This happened to many under Mao: Liu Shaoqi, Chen Boda, Jiang Qing, Lin Biao, and Hua Guofeng. Hu Yaobang, Deng's protégé, is similar. The eventual leader emerges on the basis of his own power, with military endorsement, to the surprise of most onlookers. The old generation of leaders cannot transfer whatever legitimacy they may have to the next generation, simply by selecting it as the "third echelon." Ultimately legitimacy is granted by the governed, not appointed by the rulers.

Political legitimacy is also fragile because of actual policies, decisions, and actions of the political system over the past decades. Stupidity and brutality in the cultural revolution, corruption and abuse of power, and perception of poor economic performance—these rot legitimacy.

Another issue is whether the government has enough legitimacy to enforce social and economic reforms on the urban population. For example, the government has decided not to allow inflation of food prices. Rather than go ahead with reforms of the pricing system, the government indicated that commodity prices had to be kept stable, in the interests of "social stability."[4] In an era of rising agricultural production costs, however, this means either reduced incentives for farmers or increased budgetary subsidies for the food system. Either way there is a problem. Similarly, the issues of increasing urban housing rental payments to create a system of home ownership and the question of charging tuition to university students are both very difficult. Reform of the labor system is controversial. Another unpopular policy will be the enforcement of an income tax, as the government shifts its revenue base away from enterprise profits. Long-term economic growth needs reforms in these areas, but these types of reform are dangerous politically. After December 1986, large-scale strikes and protest demonstrations are no longer inconceivable if such reforms are undertaken. Implementation of reform has been very slow, partly because of widespread opposition. To the degree that a communist leadership loses legitimacy, its ability to carry out these reforms needed for long-term economic growth becomes questionable.

While the long-term issues are serious, there is no acute crisis at this moment. With farmers building new houses and with city people buying color televisions, refrigerators and washing machines, and getting new housing, the foundation of the political system is basically stable. Cynicism, to the extent that it exists, does not easily or automatically become revolution. The question mark is in the future. Despite the draconian family planning program limiting couples to one child (with some exceptions), population growth in the future will continue to place great pressures on the system. In addition to the real pressure on resources, the population pressure creates a psychological feeling of extreme competition for scarce resources. (Chinese push vigorously to get on a bus, even when the crowds are small and there is space for everyone.) Resource constraints, pollution and ecological problems, increased needs for social infrastructure investment, and unreceptive international markets could all slow down the rapid economic growth of the past few years.

Even if growth is substantial, will it be fast enough to meet rising expectations? Increased income brings increased demand and shortages of goods. Bottlenecks multiply. For example, construction of new housing in locations away from work brings new pressures on urban public transportation. Service deteriorates and frustrations rise. Black and white television and single-door refrigerators become obsolete when color televisions and two door refrigerators enter the marketplace. The new products of course are in short supply. Some Chinese economists have, in fact, urged a slower growth rate in the economy to avoid these annoying bottlenecks. Chinese people now compare their standard of living with that in the developed countries. Even the most successful economic policies will not meet expectations. The new bottlenecks will create a revolution of rising frustrations, along with rising expectations.

China's problems in political legitimacy are not unique. Similar problems occur in other communist (and noncommunist) countries. China's political system (and most others) is resilient, and can withstand widespread loss of legitimacy without threat to political stability. If the military, police, urban factory workers, and suburban growers of farm produce are satisfied (as they appear to be), revolution is unlikely. The frustration of students, intellectuals, and artists may be embarrassing, but is of limited immediate political significance.

Nevertheless, China does have a tradition of peasant armies periodically toppling a dynasty. In addition, the experience of other communist countries shows how urban workers and intellectuals can challenge political stability. Although no socialist government has ever been completely displaced, in fact several have been overthrown. The reality is that socialism lost legitimacy (or never gained it) and was overthrown in Hungary in 1956, in Czechoslovakia in 1968, and in Poland in 1981. In each case a socialist government was continued only because of direct or indirect military support from the Soviet Union. Of course, Chinese leaders would never tolerate Soviet military support to maintain their political power, so they must never allow political legitimacy to sag to the point where regime stability is questioned.

Chinese leaders have paid close attention to these political developments in East Europe. The Hungarian revolution in 1956 had direct repercussions in China. Mao feared that the opinions expressed in the hundred flowers campaign might lead to a Hungarian-style rebellion. To preempt this possibility, the anti-rightist campaign was carried out. Potential opponents were jailed or otherwise controlled and neutralized. The Czechoslovakian rebellion in 1968 did not have the same impact in China because China already was deep into its cultural revolution.

The solidarity movement in Poland in 1980/81 came at the same time as the democracy wall movement in China. Was China starting on a similar road to popular revolution? In fact, the problems in China were certainly not as acute as in Poland. The communist government in China was home-grown, not imposed by the Soviet Red Army. Thus in China, nationalism has supported the political system, while in Poland it has contradicted the political system. Moreover, corruption was probably less prevalent in China. The Chinese leadership probably did not treat the Polish crisis as an urgent warning, but it was a background factor in their decision to undertake economic and political reforms. Some observers believe that the experience of Poland encouraged those in the Democracy Movement to begin organizing autonomous trade unions, and also hardened the attitude of the party leadership.[5] One reflection of the impact of Poland can be seen in China's new constitution, eventually adopted in December 1982. Because of the role of strikes in Poland, the new Chinese constitution banned strikes. Previous constitutions had allowed strikes.

The options for China implied by the Polish crisis were clear: 1) Follow Poland's example of martial law or repeat the anti-rightist campaign. In the aftermath of the cultural revolution, a new anti-rightist campaign would have been very unpopular. Martial law was no longer inconceivable. In Directive No. 1 in January 1987, Deng expressed support for the approach of the Polish leaders. 2) Allow the regime to lose legitimacy and tolerate the emergence of independent political movements. This was unthinkable to party leaders who never have shared power. 3) Start a major reform of the economic and political system, to regain the political legitimacy of the Communist Party. 4) Start a program of adjustment to strengthen party rule. This was the goal of Deng and his senior associates.

China's leaders recognized their political dilemma. They agreed to do something about the political situation, but they disagreed about what to do. They sensed the inherent contradiction of reform. Explaining the need for reform would weaken their own legitimacy. Promise of reform would create new expectations that could not be easily met. Some people would want immediate, drastic reform, while many would oppose reform and would allow change only at a glacial rate. Frustration and conflict were inevitable.

Perhaps for such reasons, other socialist countries have not made major reforms to improve efficiency or expand legitimacy. They have resorted to police controls instead. The government in the Soviet Union, at least before Gorbachev, seemed to be on a downward spiral, and was not reforming.

Remarkably enough, Gorbachev in January 1987 launched a program for political reform, somewhat similar to China's and for similar reasons.[6] Is world communism entering a new era of reform? If reform is successful in the Soviet Union, reform forces in China would be strengthened. It would be clear even to the most conservative hardliners that communist systems must reform. It is also clear from the dynamics in China that Gorbachev's reforms will face well-entrenched opposition.

## THE CONSERVATIVE PROGRAM

The backlash of 1987 highlights the strong position of conservative reformers. The conservative solution to China's problems is to make adjustments, improvements, and minor modifications that will strengthen the legitimacy of the existing system. As long as the government maintains domestic stability, many people will be happy. This can be combined with nationalism, economic growth, traditional authoritarianism, political apathy and cynicism, and a bit of coercion. Differences of opinion and interest would be obscured and submerged under the assertion of national unity. The state economic planners would continue to make many crucial price and wage decisions that would determine economic benefits. The state would maintain its control over sectors in society.

Some conservative reformers have an elitist, technocratic bias. Some of the new top leaders have engineering backgrounds, and might propose to engineer solutions to social problems without relying on public participation through institutionalized channels. Many were trained in the Soviet Union in the 1950s and generally accept the Soviet model of politics. They see no particular need for institutionalized participation of all those uneducated non-specialists in making decisions. Vice Premier Li Peng symbolizes this group.[7] Chinese technocrats could argue (with some validity) that economic growth in the early and middle stages of industrialization has been accomplished with authoritarian politics in South Korea, Taiwan, Singapore, and Japan.

Conservative reformers may make some significant adjustments in administration. They will strengthen the legal framework to ensure discipline, and will try to eliminate (or reduce) corruption. They will allow former cadres and their children to go into business. Creating viable career options outside of government is beneficial to both political and economic reform, even if such a policy risks criticism as abuse of power.

Conservatives will allow some separation of the functions of party and government and will encourage substantial reforms in management of economic enterprises to improve efficiency. They will seek better trained, young cadres. The conservative reform will create a "socialist democracy" under Communist Party leadership, for the vast number of laboring people, not a "bourgeois democracy" with multiple parties for the property owners.[8] This is the reform program of Deng Xiaoping. The four cardinal principles—socialism, dictatorship of the proletariat, Communist Party rule, and Marxism, Leninism, and Mao Zedong thought—limit reform to these types of adjustments that strengthen the system.

One important advantage of the conservative approach is that it might provide stability for a few years, as China goes through a potentially tense period of implementing very controversial reforms in the labor, pricing, and housing systems.

It is unlikely that conservatives would or could unleash a new cultural revolution. The Chinese people have learned a great deal from the 1960s. They embarked on the first cultural revolution with a naive enthusiasm, and only gradually discovered that it provided a new and unexcelled opportunity for violence, corruption, and privilege. This lesson was well learned. In the 1980s they have enjoyed the new policy of openness. If any leader spoke of anything like a new cultural revolution, or threatened to have "closed" policies, there would be very large-scale opposition. At a minimum, intellectuals would resist by undermining development of science and technology. In 1983, conservatives advocated an anti-spiritual pollution campaign. It was blocked after about two months. A new cultural revolution in China is as unlikely as a new

Hitler in Germany or a new Japanese military attack on Pearl Harbor. Certain aspects of the cultural revolution, such as its anti-bureaucratic, anti-intellectual, nativistic strands, might reappear in some new form.

This conservative road is generally in conformity with China's political culture and both old and recent history. Chinese culture expects government leadership. It grants legitimacy to a government that provides order, economic growth, and ceremony. Western-style elections and competitive political parties were not needed for legitimacy. The Chinese never accepted Adam Smith's philosophy that individuals interacting through free markets would create socially optimal results. They view the social problems of the West, including collapse of the family system, drugs, unemployment, and so forth as confirmation of the idea that the government must not leave the setting of social policy to an "invisible hand." Reform from above bears some similarity to the Meiji reforms in Japan in the late 1800s which the Chinese regard as successful, even though they resulted in Japanese attacks on China.

This type of reform is consistent with the traditional liberal strands of Confucianism, that call for fighting corruption and using ethics to establish good government.[9] China's conservative reform is also similar to democratic political reforms elsewhere. S. Huntington observes:

In fact, however, democratic regimes that last have seldom, if ever been instituted by mass popular action. Almost always, democracy has come as much from the top down as from the bottom up; it is as likely to be the product of oligarchy as of protest against oligarchy. The passionate dissidents from authoritarian rule and the crusaders for democratic principles, the Tom Paines of the world, do not create democratic institutions; that requires James Madisons. Those institutions come into existence through negotiations and compromises among political elites calculating their own interests and desires.[10]

Will Chinese youth resist conservative reform and continue to stage demonstrations in the future, as they did in December 1986? Not necessarily. Student movements in the United States, France, and Japan in the 1960s did not set the stage for perpetual student rebellion. Throughout the world, student uprisings may have contributed to conservative backlashes, and the following generations of students have become less interested in protest.

While there is much support for a conservative approach, there are problems with it also. At present, support for a conservative program seems to be greater among older people. The conservative forces can only lose power as time proceeds, but will continue to have a base of support in the bureaucracy and among those craving stability. The values of today's youth after twenty years is an important unknown.

Another potential weakness is that it might not bring enthusiasm and unlock the creative energies of intellectuals, entrepreneurs, workers, and political leaders that are needed for sustained economic growth. Using a combination of apathy and traditional acceptance of authority creates a favorable environment for "local emperors" who only undermine further the legitimacy of the central system through corruption and incompetence. Thus the conservative approach may reinforce short-term legitimacy at the expense of long-term problems.

The conservative road would probably be unpopular in Hong Kong. The successful integration of a vibrant Hong Kong into the Chinese polity in 1997 would be especially difficult under these conditions. Hong Kong's entrepreneurs would take their capital elsewhere, leaving behind a stagnant, overcrowded city. This, of course, would render the Taiwan problem even more unsolvable. (This dynamic may have already begun.)

Moreover, this type of social and political stability is not permanent. In South Korea and Taiwan, there have been demonstrations or other demands for increased democratic participation. The conservative reaction to these demands could well be repression, as it has been in South Korea. This would simply take China down the road of Soviet-style politics. This is by no means impossible.

## RADICAL REFORMS

The radical reformers lost power in the backlash of 1987. Their outlook had been to demand more than minor adjustments to strengthen the system. They proposed, instead, to change it. Reform would give people, especially the young, a sense of choice and an ability to make effective input into the policymaking process. In the West, the crucial feature that gives this feeling is having electoral competition between different parties. Because people feel the choice between parties has been made democratically according to appropriate procedures, they accept the political leaders and policies as legitimate, even if they disagree with the outcome. This structure of legitimacy gives political strength and stability to Western governments, despite the superficial appearance of electoral chaos and widespread reality of government incompetence, cronyism, and corruption, just as in mature socialist systems. Indeed, electoral legitimacy gives great stability to the political systems of India and Mexico, despite very deep social and economic problems.

Is there any possibility that China could develop a competitive party system of this sort? Some Chinese advocate this. Wang Ruowang, criticized in January 1987, had urged that multiparty politics was the crucial issue.[11] The student demonstrations, in a vague way, had this objective. One of their demands was for their own representatives in their student unions, as well as in people's congresses.

Nevertheless, it is very difficult and risky to establish such a party system. Would China be well served with an electoral system and parliamentary system like those in South Korea, the Philippines, or Bangladesh? In those countries, elected officials have not gained full legitimacy, and the military is still very powerful.

Would the Chinese political system be able to withstand the centrifugal forces of a political competition? Even Chinese reformers are doubtful. One reform leader commented,

> If left to their own devices, the Chinese people would tear each other to bits. ... We all saw that during the cultural revolution. Democratic foundations have to be built gradually. If you handed democracy to the Chinese people now, they wouldn't know what to do with it.[12]

Some of my friends (including some who have studied in the United States) share this fear that chaos is a real risk.

Of course China would never have a political system that is a simple copy of Western political forms. Whatever China does, it will always have a distinctly Chinese approach. If politics become more open, many traditional forms are likely to reappear. Chinese party politics will certainly have elements of lineage, factionalism, and regionalism. The key issue, to use Samuel Huntington's vocabulary, is whether the political institutions can handle effectively the increased demands for participation. If not, political stagnation could result.[13]

It is surprising that when Chinese talk about the risks of chaos, they seem to forget the potential of unity. China has ethnic, linguistic, and cultural unity. Ethnic minorities are only about 6 percent of the population. There is no longer an established feudal landlord class. The economic differences between rich and poor individuals and regions are, by world standards, not particularly large. The central state has existed for over two thousand years. There is no need for "nation building" as in many new countries, even though there may be a need for new political values.

The cultural revolution is sometimes used as a reminder of the risks of chaos. But that was a very unusual situation, where the adored leader asked people to be chaotic. Chaos did not happen spontaneously. China should be better able to cope with the centrifugal forces of political competition than, say, India, Switzerland, or Germany, but there would be a complicated learning period, as voters and leaders gradually learn new roles. China has not developed the culture or institutions of tolerance between conflicting ethnic groups, religions, and economic classes that Europe and North America evolved over centuries.

One important obstacle to developing democratic values may well be in the structure of authority, shaped by cultural values and child rearing patterns. If this is true, then political change could come only gradually as culture and child rearing patterns change generation by generation. (In point of fact, the new single child families do have some new patterns in child rearing, the implications of which are not yet clear.)

If China were to have a more competitive political system, the communist party would certainly remain dominant, at least for many years, just as the PRI has been dominant in Mexico. It might lose some local elections, and a national election from time to time. That happened to the Congress Party in India once. In the long run, such competition could strengthen the party by forcing it to work better, and would give it clear legitimacy to enforce new and demanding policies. One has only to think of the mayor of Shanghai, struggling to reply to students' questions about the basis of his legitimacy. He would be far stronger if he could say to students that he had been elected by a majority of all voters.

It is possible that the framework of the National People's Congress could provide the context in which political competition emerges. The new law for the spring 1987 elections does allow for some competition between candidates.

Robert Dahl has observed that democracy has evolved most often from systems that had public contestation before extensive participation.[14] From this perspective, more open discussion and eventually formal voting within the National People's Congress and the party's Central Committee could be an important transitional stage in China's political reform.

In early 1987, after the conservative backlash began, this scenario of competitive elections had no public support. The most important of the cardinal principles of the political system was the unchallenged leadership of the Communist Party. Its right to rule is similar to the divine right of European monarchs of another era. No one could suggest an alternative in early 1987. A Chinese article warned:

Can a multiparty politics be exercised in China? As everyone is aware, the multiparty political system in capitalist countries is determined by bourgeois parties competing for doing each other down. Different bourgeois parties abuse each other, one coming to power, and the other down. This seems quite "democratic," but not one of them represents the interests of the working people. Is there a need to introduce such a multiparty political system in China? Its introduction in China could only cause confusion and bring about a split. In such cases it would be impossible to realize modernization.[15]

But sometimes events move faster than expected. China in 1986 was unthinkable ten years earlier. The Chinese are well aware of the benefits of competition. Their athletic teams thrive on international competition. They are setting up several airlines, to generate competition that will improve service.[16] Economist Sun Xiaoliang commented, "The new system is characterized by competition."[17]

Why is the same principle not applicable to political parties? Would not competition between parties improve the service of parties, in a similar manner? Moreover, the Communist Party has put forward the slogan "one country, two systems" to describe the proposed method of integrating Hong Kong and Taiwan with mainland China. If a country can have two systems, why not two or more parties?

There are, of course, many obstacles to this scenario. A large portion of the population still has a traditional political culture. They expect government to be strong and to impose unity. This will ensure stability. Political competition produces anxiety because it reminds people of instability and chaos. Western-style democratization will not be feasible until there has been a substantial change in the country's political culture. The problems of vested interests among cadres and urban residents remain serious. Most importantly, the senior cadres find the idea of inter-party competition to be abhorrent.

The most optimistic forecast for successful democratic reform is at best several decades. China will first have five to ten years of conservative adjustments. After that, there may be results from experiments about political reform in test cities, and the next political succession will be complete. How reform could proceed after that point is difficult to predict. By then, China will have a new generation of leaders. Each generation of leaders can change, even if only a small amount. Everywhere, people in power give up power only slowly, if they can do so. That is one clear implication of the way senior officials, upset with proposals that they retire, insisted on forcing the resignation of Hu Yaobang instead. Ten years will be needed for today's octogenarians to pass from the scene. Thirty years will be needed before today's twenty-year-olds are in positions of power and able to implement policies more consistent with their values. An important issue will be what their values will be at that time. In most countries that have made a transition to democracy, this type of gradual change was required so that all leaders and interests could make their adjustments peacefully.[18]

The pace and depth of reform in China will be influenced by external events. A factor that may speed things up is political change in Taiwan. In 1986, Taiwan started a remarkable democratization process. President Chiang Ching-kuo personally initiated the change. Martial law was ended, and an opposition party, the Democratic Progressive Party, was allowed to form, and compete in elections in December 1986. It elected roughly 15 percent of the contested seats in the legislative yuan and national assembly.[19] The reasons for Taiwan's dramatic political reform are related to the passing of an old generation and the democratic political values of the younger generation, many of whose leaders have studied in the United States and were finding Taiwan's authoritarian political system inappropriate. Taiwan's action may have been related to discussion of political reform in the mainland, but it could encourage the communist leadership to take similar policies. China's youth are well aware of these developments in Taiwan. Taiwan's economic success is one factor that inspired the mainland's economic reform; perhaps if Taiwan moves toward a more democratic political system, there will be a similar learning and competition.

Likewise, the political processes in Hong Kong can have a bearing on China's internal politics. China now seems to be discouraging direct elections in a multiparty environment in Hong Kong, partly for this reason.

The issue of reform in the Soviet Union will also impinge on reform in China. The discussion of reform in China may be contributed to Gorbachev's reform efforts. If Gorbachev is successful, China would not want to fall far behind.

If China moves toward deeper reform, there will be controversy, hesitation, and occasional reversals. Participatory politics may slow economic growth, as powerful groups demand special treatment.[20] Open competition will be distasteful to many because it will remind them of chaos. Corruption and machine politics do, of course, flourish in democratic electoral politics just as they can in an authoritarian environment. The advantages of democracy will not be obvious to everyone. There will always be some opposition to democratic reforms, if and when they are adopted.

Some may be disappointed with the view that reform in China may take decades. This is, however, in accordance with the experience in other political sytstems. The transformation from authoritarian to democratic systems and the expansion of adult suffrage to all adults took several centuries in England and decades in Sweden, Norway, and even the United States. In the southern states of the United States, political democracy has been slow in coming to Blacks.

Worse than a slow transition to democracy is an unsuccessful one. In some countries, such as Germany, Italy, and Japan, prewar democratic transformations failed, and dictatorship, war, and defeat resulted. The transition to democracy was finally made in the context of a U.S. military occupation after these traumas. China's cultural revolution was, in a sense, an analogous social trauma. China will be cautious to avoid flaws in constitutional structure that would allow repetition.

Nevertheless, the possibility of chaos and military dictatorship should also be considered. China inevitably faces many challenges in the future. Students might continue to demonstrate or turn to terrorism or sabotage. Farmers might find production incentives lacking and refuse to supply cities with commodities. The global economy can turn protectionist and foreign companies may decide that there are too many bureaucratic problems and risks in investing in China. Chinese may become more annoyed about the domestic impact of international culture, values, and commerce. The economy could falter and workers might be tempted to join in demonstrations next time. Taiwan could try to become an independent country. The central political leadership may become highly factionalized and unable to select leaders and policies. The leaders selected may not be considered legitimate. All of these are real possibilities.

Moreover, the long-term commitment of young generations to democratic values must be an open question. Chinese youth, as youth elsewhere, have in the past enthusiastically supported violent, authoritarian politics. Marx, Lenin, and Mao are still available to China's next young generation of radicals who may be upset by the emerging class differentiation. A new radical movement could emerge.

With all these potential tensions, the breakdown of social order is possible, and the establishment of martial law is conceivable. Endemic domestic violence throughout South Asia and Africa is a constant reminder of the fragile nature of political order.

The history of democratic countries shows that democratic reform is at best a difficult challenge. The history of socialist countries shows an even bigger challenge. In the seventy years of Marxist-Leninist governments, none has become democratic, as understood by the West.

From these perspectives, China's current reforms should be evaluated not by whether they bring full democracy now or in a year or three. The reforms now underway will at best constitute adjustments to improve the efficiency of the existing communist authoritarian system. From a long-term perspective, these conservative adjustments have already legitimated deeper discussion of reform, and inspired broad support and demand for more change. The crucial question is whether current reforms also contribute to a twenty- to forty-year process of continual reform of the political structure. From this perspective, there are reasons to be optimistic.

## NOTES

1. Liang Heng and Judith Shapiro, *After the Nightmare* (New York: Knopf, 1986), pp. 74–98.

2. Richard Braungart and Margaret Braungart, "Conceptual and methodological approaches to studying life course and generational politics," in Richard Braungart and Margaret Braungart (eds.), *Research in Political Sociology*, vol. 1 (Greenwich, CT: JAI Press, 1985), p. 276.

3. Vladimir Shapentokh, "Attitude and behavior of Soviet youth in the 1970s and 1980s: the mysterious variable in Soviet politics," in Richard Braungart and Margaret Braungart (eds.), *Research in Political Sociology*, vol 2 (Greenwich, CT: JAI Press, 1986), pp. 199–200.

4. "Control of prices the key to stability," *China Daily* (Jan. 16, 1987), p. 1.

5. Robin Munro, "Chen Erjin and the Chinese Democracy Movement," in Chen Erjin, *China: Crossroads Socialism* (London: Verso, 1984), p. 14.

6. "Gorbachev proposes changes that would challenge the elite," *Christian Science Monitor* (Jan. 28, 1987), p. 1.

7. Dong Xusheng, "Li Peng and the Soviet Connection," *China Spring Digest* (Jan./Feb. 1987), pp. 9–12.

8. Gu Chunde, "A brief discourse on the differences in nature between socialist democracy and bourgeois democracy," *China Law Journal* (Jan. 16, 1987); FBIS (Jan. 30, 1987), pp. K 14–17.

9. William Theodore de Bary, *The Liberal Tradition in China* (New York: Columbia University Press, 1983).

10. Samuel Huntington, "Will more countries become democratic?" In Samuel Huntington and Joseph Nye (eds.), *Global Dilemmas* (Cambridge, MA: Harvard University Press, 1986), pp. 269–70.

11. Zhang Zhenlu, "See the essence of bourgeois liberalization from Wang Ruowang's remarks," *People's Daily* (Jan. 18, 1987), p. 4; FBIS (Jan. 21, 1987), p. K 25.

12. Heng and Shapiro, *After the Nightmare*, p. 93.

13. Samuel Huntington, *Political Order in Changing Societies* (New Haven: Yale University Press, 1968).

14. Robert Dahl, *Polyarchy* (New Haven: Yale, 1971).

15. Zhang Zhenlu, "See the essence of bourgeois liberalization from Wang Ruowang's remarks," *People's Daily* (Jan. 18, 1987), p. 4; FBIS (Jan. 21, 1987), p. K 25.

16. "China to establish six new airlines," *China Daily* (Feb. 16, 1987), p. 3.

17. "Big risk in slowing reforms," *China Daily* (Jan. 13, 1987), p. 4.

18. Samuel Huntington, "Will more countries become democratic?" pp. 253–279.

19. John Copper, "Political developments in Taiwan in 1986," *China News Analysis*, no. 1327 (Jan. 15, 1987).

20. Erich Weede, "Catch-up, distributional coalitions and government as determinants of economic growth or decline in industrialized democracies," *British Journal of Sociology*, 37:2 (1986), pp. 194–220.

# Bibliography

Berrington, Hugh. "British government, the paradox of strength." In Dennis Kavanagh and Gillian Peele (eds.) *Comparative Government and Politics.* Boulder: Westview, 1984.

Bo Guili. "The function of local government in managing the economy, and the reform of local government institutions." *Political Science Research,* no. 3 (1986), pp. 42–45. Available in Benedict Stavis (ed.), "Reform of China's political system." *Chinese Law and Government,* 20:1 (Spring 1987).

Braungart, Richard, and Margaret Braungart. "Conceptual and methodological approaches to studying life course and generational politics." In Richard Braungart and Margaret Braungart (eds.), *Research in Political Sociology,* Vol. 1. Greenwich, CT: JAI Press, 1985.

Byrnes, Robert. "Change in the Soviet political system: Limits and likelihoods." *Review of Politics* (Oct. 1984), pp. 502–15.

Chang Chieh-feng. "Document No. 1 to 6 reveal current situation." *Hong Kong Pai Hsing,* no. 138 (Feb. 17, 1987), p. K 15.

Chang Hsing. "Princes' party?" *Ming Pao* (Dec. 30, 1985), p. 5; FBIS (Dec. 31, 1985), p. W 1.

Chen, David. "CPC secretariat holds political reform meeting." *South China Morning Post* (Aug. 13, 1986), p. 16; FBIS (Aug. 13, 1986), p. W 5.

Chen Qiren. "Socialist theory, practice and commodity economy." *Shijie Jingji Wenhui,* no. 5 (1986), pp. 30–36.

Cheng Hsiang. "Tentative analysis of discussion concerning reform of the political structure." *Wen Wei Bao* (July 21, 1986); FBIS (July 24, 1986), p. W 1.

———. "News from Beidaihe." *Wen Wei Bao* (Aug. 8, 1986), p. 2; FBIS (Aug. 11, 1986), p. W 1.

Chuang Ming. "Zhao Ziyang receives instruction in time of danger to save a desparate situation." *Hong Kong Ching Pao* (Feb. 10, 1987), pp. 27–29; FBIS (Feb. 12, 1987), p. K 5.

Clarke, Christopher M. "Rejuvenation, reorganization and the dilemmas of modernization in post-Deng China." *Journal of International Affairs*, 39:2 (Winter, 1986), pp. 119–132.

Cohen, Jerome Alan, and Ta-Kuang Chang. "New foreign investment provisions." *Chinese Business Review* (Jan./Feb. 1987), pp. 11–15.

Colton, Timothy. *Dilemma of Reform in the Soviet Union*. New York: Council on Foreign Relations, 1984.

Copper, John. "Political developments in Taiwan in 1986." *China News Analysis*, no. 1327 (Jan. 15, 1987).

Cracraft, James. "A Soviet turning point." *Bulletin of the Atomic Scientists* (Feb. 1986), pp. 8–12.

Dahl, Robert. *Polyarchy*. New Haven: Yale, 1971.

de Bary, William Theodore. *The Liberal Tradition in China*. New York: Columbia University Press, 1973.

Deng Xiaoping. "Uphold the four cardinal principles." *Selected Works of Deng Xiaoping (1975–1982)*. Beijing: Foreign Languages Press, 1984.

Dittmer, Lowell. "The 12th Congress of the Communist Party of China." *China Quarterly* no. 93 (March 1983), pp. 108–124.

Domes, Jurgen. "New policies in the communes: Notes on rural societal structure in China, 1976–81." *Journal of Asian Studies* 41:2 (Feb. 1982), pp. 253–268.

Dong Xusheng. "China: toward rational totalitarianism?" *China Spring Digest* (Jan./Feb. 1987), pp. 54–62.

———. "Who's who in Deng and Chen factions." *China Spring Digest* (Jan./Feb. 1987), pp. 18–24.

———. "Li Peng and the Soviet Connection." *China Spring Digest* (Jan./Feb. 1987), pp. 9–12.

Fang Lizhi. A speech to Beijing reporters on Sept. 3, 1986. Published in Society (Shehui Bao, Oct. 28, 1986), and reprinted in *The Nineties* (Feb. 1987), pp. 52–54.

———. *Bright Daily* (Nov. 1986); available in *Beijing Review*, no. 50 (Dec. 15, 1986), pp. 16–17.

———. Speeches at Jiaotong University, Nov. 15, 1986, and Tongji University, Nov. 18, 1986. *China Spring*, no. 45 (March 1987), p. 11–33. Portions of the Jiaotong speech were published as "A Chinese Tom Paine speaks out on democracy," in the *Washington Post* (Jan. 18, 1987), p. C 1. Translations of the Jiaotong and Tongji speeches are available in *China Spring Digest*, 1:2 (March/April 1987), pp. 12–25, 26–29.

"Fang Lizhi's Biography." *China Spring Digest* (March/April, 1987), p. 2.

["Professor] Fang Lizhi, just back from Europe." *World Economic Herald* (Nov. 24, 1986); FBIS (Dec. 19, 1986), p. K 13.

Fewsmich, Joseph. "Special economic zones in the PRC." *Problems of Communism*, 35:6 (Nov./Dec. 1986), pp. 78–85.

Friederich, Carl, and Zbigniew Brzezinski. *Totalitarian Dictatorship and Autocracy*. Cambridge, MA: Harvard University Press, 1956.

Friedman, Edward. "The societal obstacle to China's socialist transition: state capitalism or feudal fascism." In Victor Nee and David Mozingo (eds.),

*State and Society in Contemporary China.* Ithaca, NY: Cornell University Press, 1983, pp. 148–71.

Gao Ming. On Bukharin's theory of State Capitalism and the transition period. Fudan University, International Politics Department, MA essay, 1985.

Garside, Roger. *Coming Alive, China After Mao.* New York: McGraw Hill, 1981.

Gates, Millicent Anne, and E. Bruce Geelhoed. *The Dragon and the Snake.* Philadelphia: University of Pennsylvania Press, 1986.

Ge Sheng. "Fang Lizhi—a model of Chinese intellectual." *China Spring Digest* (March/April 1987), p. 9.

Goldman, Merle. *China's Intellectuals: Advise and Dissent.* Cambridge, MA: Harvard University Press, 1981.

Goodman, David. *Beijing Street Voices: The Poetry and Politics of China's Democracy Movement.* Boston: M. Boyars, 1981.

———. "The National CCP conference of Sept. 1985 and China's leadership change." *China Quarterly* no. 105 (March 1986), pp. 123–130.

Gu Chunde. "A brief discourse on the differences in nature between socialist democracy and bourgeois democracy." *China Law Journal* (Jan. 16, 1987); FBIS (Jan. 30, 1987), pp. K 14–17.

Hartford, Kathleen. "Socialist agriculture is dead: long live socialist agriculture! Organizational transformations in rural China." in Perry and Wong, *The Political Economy of Reform in Post-Mao China.*

Hood, Marlowe. "Anti-liberalization drive reportedly opposed." *South China Morning Post* (Feb. 23, 1987), p. 8; FBIS (Feb. 24, 1987), p. K 6.

———. "Serious alarm among foreign business community." *South China Morning Post* (Feb. 26, 1987), p. 8; FBIS (Feb. 26, 1987), p. K 22.

Hsiao Chang. "The cause and effect of student demonstrations in December." *Zheng Ming,* no. 111 (Jan. 1, 1987), pp. 12–13; FBIS (Jan. 5, 1987), pp. K 9–10.

Hsueh Mu-ch'iao. *China's Socialist Economy.* Beijing: Foreign Languages Press, 1981.

Huan Guocang. "China's opening to the West." *Problems of Communism,* 35:6 (Nov./Dec. 1986), pp. 59–77.

Huang Yang-lieh. "Hu Yaobang will succeed Li Xiannian as President of the PRC; Central Committee issues documents on Hu's mistakes." *Ming Pao* (Jan. 26, 1987), p. 2; FBIS (Jan. 27, 1987), p. K 5.

Huntington, Samuel. "Will more countries become democratic?" In Samuel Huntington and Joseph Nye (eds.), *Global Dilemmas.* Cambridge; MA: Harvard University Press, 1986, pp. 269–70.

———. *Political Order in Changing Societies.* New Haven: Yale University Press, 1968.

Jones, William (ed.). "Civil law in China." *Chinese Law and Government,* 18:3–4 (Fall/Winter, 1985/86).

Kirkpatrick, Jeane. *Dictatorships and Double Standards.* New York: Simon and Schuster, 1982.

Kuang Pi-hua. "Questions concerning who will replace Zhao, and the mystery of Hua's resignation." *Hong Kong Kuang Chiao Ching,* no. 173 (Feb. 16, 1987), pp. 6–9; FBIS (Feb. 20, 1987), p. K 8.

Lardy, Nicholas. *Agriculture in China's Modern Economic Development.* New York: Cambridge University Press, 1983.

Li Honglin. "How to make socialist democracy a reality." *World Economic Herald* (June 2, 1986). Available in Benedict Stavis (ed.), "Reform of China's political system." *Chinese Law and Government,* 20:1 (Spring 1987).

Li Jiapeng. "Building of democracy as viewed from the overall scheme of modernization." *People's Daily* (Feb. 23, 1987), p. 5; FBIS (Feb. 27, 1987), pp. K 2–5.

Li Kejing. "China's political restructuring and the development of political science." *Social Sciences in China,* 7:3 (Sept. 1986), pp. 9–24.

Liang Heng and Judith Shapiro. *After the Nightmare.* New York: Knopf, 1986.

———. "In China, the year—and claws—of the tiger." *New York Times* (March 8, 1986), Section I, p. 27.

———. "China: How much freedom?" *New York Review of Books,* 32:6 (Oct. 24, 1985), pp. 14–16.

Liu Binyan. "People or monsters." In Perry Link (ed.), *People or Monsters, and other Stories.* Bloomington: Indiana University Press, 1983.

Lo Ping. "Chen Yun capitalizes on Hu Yaobang and Zhao Ziyang's vulnerable point." *Zheng Ming,* no. 99 (Jan. 1, 1986), pp. 6–8; FBIS (Jan. 6, 1986), pp. W 3–8.

———. "Two shocking major cases." *Zheng Ming* (July 1, 1986), pp. 6–7; FBIS (July 10, 1986), pp. W 1–3.

———. "Note on a northern journey—Deng Xiaoping criticizes Chen Yun at meeting." *Zheng Ming,* no. 108 (Oct. 1, 1986), pp. 8–12; FBIS (Oct. 9, 1986), p. K 15.

———. "Sudden rise of calls for Qiao Shi to become General Secretary." *Zheng Ming,* no. 108 (Oct. 1, 1986), pp. 6–8; FBIS (Oct. 10, 1986), pp. K 1–2.

———. "Note on a northern journey—reformists suffer setback for the first time." *Zheng Ming,* no. 109 (Nov. 1, 1986), pp. 6–10; FBIS (Nov. 18, 1986), pp. K 1–9.

———. "Note on a northern journey—A Yao Wenyuan type hatchet man has gone on the stage—dispute on the political reform between those in power and the public." *Zheng Ming,* no. 110 (Dec. 1, 1986), pp. 9–12; FBIS (Dec. 12, 1986), p. K 13.

———. "Disputes inside the party between the faction which wants Deng to stay and the faction which wants Deng to retire." *Zheng Ming,* no. 110 (Dec. 1, 1986), pp. 6–8; FBIS (Dec. 4, 1986), p. K 9.

———. "The Huangpu Jiang roars on." *Zheng Ming,* no. 111 (Jan. 1, 1987); FBIS (Jan. 8, 1987), p. K 11.

———. "The truth of the Hu Yaobang incident." *Zheng Ming,* no. 112 (Feb. 1, 1987), pp. 6–10; FBIS (Jan. 29, 1987), p. K 6.

———. "The drive to overthrow Hu has intensified to a major crisis." *Zheng Ming,* no. 113 (March 1, 1987), pp. 6–10; FBIS (March 3, 1987), pp. K 1–8.

Lu Tzu-chien. "Hu Yaobang's five mistakes." *Ming Pao* (Jan. 31, 1987), p. 2; FBIS (Feb. 2, 1987), p. K 1.

MacDonald, Lawrence. "Assembly preceding Shanghai demonstrations noted." *AFP* (Dec. 23, 1986); FBIS (Dec. 23, 1986), p. O 2.

Moody, Peter. "The romance of the Three Kingdoms and popular Chinese political culture." *Review of Politics*, 37:2 (April 1975), pp. 175–199.

Munro, Robin. "Chen Erjin and the Chinese Democracy Movement." In Chen Erjin (ed.), *China: Crossroads Socialism*. London: Verso, 1984, pp. 6–15.

Nathan, Andrew. "A factionalism model of CCP Politics." *China Quarterly*, no. 53 (Jan.-March 1973), pp. 34–66.

———. *Chinese Democracy*. New York: Knopf, 1985.

Naughton, Barry. "False starts and second wind: Financial reforms in China's industrial system." In Perry and Wong, *The Political Economy of Reform in Post-Mao China*.

Oksenberg, Michel. "The exit pattern from Chinese politics and its implications." *China Quarterly*, no. 67 (Sept. 1976), pp. 501–518.

Olson, Mancur. *The Rise and Decline of Nations: Economic Growth, Stagflation, and Social Rigidities*. New Haven: Yale University Press, 1982.

Pai Yen. "Drastic actions taken by Hu Qiaomu and Deng Liqun to oppose bourgeois liberalizations." *Zheng Ming*, no. 113 (March 1, 1987), pp. 16–18; FBIS (March 5, 1987), p. K 12.

Peng Zhen. "The four cardinal principles are the guiding thought of the constitution." Speech to the 19th meeting of the 6th NPC Standing Committee, Jan. 21, 1987, Central TV. FBIS (Jan. 27, 1987), p. K 17.

Perry, Elizabeth and Christine Wong. *The Political Economy of Reform in Post-Mao China*. Cambridge: Harvard Council on East Asian Studies, 1985.

Pu Xingzu. "Increase the authority of the legislative bodies." *Political Science Research*, no. 2 (1986), pp. 15–17. Available in Benedict Stavis (ed.), "Reform of China's political system." *Chinese Law and Government*, 20:1 (Spring 1987).

Pye, Lucian. *The Spirit of Chinese Politics*. Cambridge, MA: MIT Press, 1968.

———. *The Dynamics of Chinese Politics*. Cambridge, MA: Oelgeschlager, Gunn & Hain, 1981.

———. "On Chinese pragmatism." *China Quarterly*, no. 106 (June 1986), pp. 207–234.

Raddock, David. *Political Behavior of Adolescents in China: The Cultural Revolution in Kwangchow*. Tucson: University of Arizona Press, 1977.

Rosen, Stanley. "Guangzhou's democracy movement in cultural revolution perspective." *China Quarterly*, no. 101 (March 1985), pp. 1–31.

———. "Prosperity, Privatization, and China's youth." *Problems of Communism*, 34:2 (March-April 1985), pp. 1–29.

Rubin, Vitaly, A. *Individual and State in Ancient China*. New York: Columbia University Press, 1976.

Saich, Tony. "Party building since Mao-A question of style?" in Neville Maxwell and Bruce McFarlane, *China's Changed Road to Development*. Oxford: Pergamon Press, 1984, pp. 149–167.

Seymour, James. *The Fifth Modernization: China's Human Rights Movement*. Standfordville, NY: Human Rights Publishing Group, 1980.

———. *China's Rights Annals no. 1*. Armonk, NY: Sharpe, 1985.

Shambaugh, David (ed.). "Zhao Ziyang's 'Sichuan Experience.'" *Chinese Law and Government*, 15:1 (Spring 1982), pp. 3–13.

Shapentokh, Vladimir. "Attitude and behavior of Soviet youth in the 1970's and

1980's: The mysterious variable in Soviet politics." In Richard Braungart and Margaret Braungart (eds.), *Research in Political Sociology*, vol. 2. Greenwich, CT: JAI Press, 1986.

Shapiro, Sidney. *Experiment in Sichuan, A Report on Economic Reform*. Peking: New World Press, 1981.

Shirk, Susan. *Competitive Comrades*. Berkeley: University of California Press, 1982.

———. "The politics of industrial reform," in Perry and Wong, *The Political Economy of Reform in Post-Mao China*.

Shue, Vivienne. "The fate of the commune." *Modern China* 10:3 (1984), pp. 259–283.

Slider, Darrell. Social experiments and Soviet policy making. Ph.D. dissertation, Yale, 1981.

Solinger, Dorothy J. "Industrial reform: decentralization, differentiation, and the difficulties." *Journal of International Affairs*, 39:2 (Winter, 1986), pp. 105–118.

Solomon, Richard. *Mao's Revolution and the Chinese Political Culture*. Berkeley: University of California, 1971.

Stavis, Benedict. "Reform of China's political system." *Chinese Law and Government*, 20:1 (Spring 1987).

———. "Some initial results of China's new agricultural policies." *World Development*, 13:12 (Dec. 1985), pp. 1299–1305.

Su Shaozhi. "The precondition for reform of political institutions is getting rid of feudal pernicious influences." *People's Daily* (Aug. 15, 1986). Available in Benedict Stavis (ed.), "Reform of China's political system." *Chinese Law and Government*, 20:1 (Spring 1987).

Thurston, Anne. *Enemies of the People*. New York: Knopf, 1986.

Tong, James (ed.). "Underground journals in China." *Chinese Law and Government*, 13:3–4 (Fall/Winter 1980/81).

Wan Li. "Making decision making more democratic and scientific is an important part of reform of the political system." *People's Daily* (Aug. 15, 1986). Available in Benedict Stavis (ed.), "Reform of China's political system." *Chinese Law and Government*, 20:1 (Spring 1987).

Wang Bingzhang. "Cause and consequence." *China Spring Digest*, (March/April 1987), pp. 39–41.

Wang Huning. "Moving towards a political system with higher efficiency and more democracy." *World Economic Herald*, Shanghai (July 21, 1986). Available in Benedict Stavis (ed.), "Reform of China's political system." *Chinese Law and Government*, 20:1 (Spring 1987).

Wang Ruoshui. "On the Marxist philosophy of man." *Wenhui Bao* (July 17, 18, 1986); FBIS (July 23, 1986), p. K 7–13; (July 24, 1986), pp. K 1–8.

Wang Zhaoguo. "On political structural reform." *Red Flag*, no. 17 (Sept. 1986), pp. 6–15; FBIS (Sept. 22, 1986), pp. K 8–21.

Watson, Andrew. "New structures in the organization of Chinese agriculture: a variable model." *Pacific Affairs*, 57:4 (Winter 1984–85), pp. 621–45.

Weede, Erich. "Catch-up, distributional coalitions and government as determinants of economic growth or decline in industrialized democracies." *British Journal of Sociology*, 37:2 (1986), pp. 194–220.

Wei Haibo. "Reform of the political system and political democratization." *Legal*

*Studies*, no. 10 (1986). Available in Benedict Stavis (ed.), "Reform of China's political system." *Chinese Law and Government*, 20:1 (Spring 1987).

Womack, Brantly. "Electoral Reform in China." *Chinese Law and Government*, 15:3–4 (Fall-Winter 1982–83).

Xu Jingyu. "All Chinese armies are turned into group armies." *Liaowang Overseas*, no. 40 (Oct. 6, 1986), pp. 16–17; FBIS (Oct. 15, 1986), p. K 11.

Xu Zhaoming. "The changing function of government." *Political Science Research*, no. 5 (1986), pp. 53–57. Available in Benedict Stavis (ed.), "Reform of China's political system." *Chinese Law and Government*, 20:1 (Spring 1987).

Yan Jiaqi. "Our current political system and the goals of reform." *Liberation Daily* [Shanghai] (Aug. 13, 1986). Available in Benedict Stavis (ed.), "Reform of China's political system." *Chinese Law and Government*, 20:1 (Spring 1987).

———. "To develop, China must adopt an overall approach of cultural opening up." *Liaowang Overseas*, no. 40 (Oct. 6, 1986), p. 12: FBIS (Oct. 10, 1986), pp. K 5–7.

———. "Yan Jiaqi proposes that 'People's Congresses' be changed to People's Assemblies in the 1990's." *Zhongguo tongxun she* (Sept. 11, 1987); FBIS (Sept. 19, 1986), p. K 20.

Yan Mei-ning. "Further comments on Hu." *Hong Kong Standard* (Feb. 8, 1987), p. 9; FBIS (Feb. 9, 1987), p. K 5.

Young, Graham. "Control and style: Discipline Inspection Commission since the 11th Congress." *China Quarterly* no. 97 (March 1984).

Zeng Shiping. "On reforming the foundation of China's political institutions." *Political Research*, no. 1 (1986); pp. 26–34. Available in Benedict Stavis (ed.), "Reform of China's political system." *Chinese Law and Government*, 20:1 (Spring 1987).

Zhang Gang. "How and why is economic reform failing." *China Spring Digest*, May/June 1987, pp. 3–19.

Zhang Youyu. "Reform of the political system and the division of the work of party and government." *Bright Daily* (Oct. 29, 1986). Available in Benedict Stavis (ed.), "Reform of China's political system." *Chinese Law and Government*, 20:1 (Spring 1987).

Zhang Zhenlu. "See the essence of bourgeois liberalization from Wang Ruowang's remarks." *People's Daily* (Jan. 18, 1987), p. 4; FBIS (Jan. 21, 1987), p. K 25.

Zhao Ziyang. "Report on the work of government." *Beijing Review*, no. 16 (April 20, 1987), pp. xvi-xvii.

Zhi Mu. "Strengthening the people's congress is the fundamental way to develop socialist democracy." *World Economic Herald* (Aug. 2, 1986). Available in Benedict Stavis (ed.), "Reform of China's political system." *Chinese Law and Government*, 20:1 (Spring 1987).

Zhou Mianwei. "The right to use the slogans of democracy, liberty, and human rights does not belong only to the bourgeoisie." *Daily Worker* (Aug. 11, 1986), p. 4; FBIS (Aug. 19, 1986), p. K 5.

# *Index*

agriculture, 16, 82–3, 130
Anhui, 16, 95, 96
Aristotle, 67, 70
Arkush, David, viii-ix
authoritarian, 67, 73, 122, 129, 130, 136, 143

banking system, 42
bankruptcy, 41–2, 81, 85, 96, 121
Beidaihe, 11, 12, 67, 89, 95
Beijing, 90, 102, 103
Beijing University and students, 30–1, 90, 91, 97, 102, 103, 115
bourgeois liberalization, 5, 111, 114, 115, 116, 117, 118, 119, 120, 122, 123, 132
Boxer Rebellion, 117
British Broadcasting Corporation, 97
Bukharin, 14
bureaucracy, 9–10, 11, 17, 84

cadres, cadre system, 47, 131, 137
Central Advisory Commission, 47, 116
Central Committee, 10, 47
chaos, 18, 28, 68, 69, 95, 101, 140, 142, 143
checks and balances, 52

Chen Boda, 133
Chen Junsheng, 118
Chen Yi, 23
Chen Yuan, 23
Chen Yun, 11, 12, 74, 99
Chiang Kai-shek, 25
China Science and Technology, University, 91, 96
Christmas, 29
civil liberties, 58
commodity economy, 42
communes, 16, 54
Communist Party (of China), vii, 1, 2, 9, 19, 23, 25, 26, 29, 30, 31, 40, 45, 47, 51, 55, 56, 57, 59, 60, 75, 84, 93, 95, 113, 121, 130, 131, 136, 137, 141, 142
Communist Youth League, 111, 113
Confucius, 26, 67, 68, 69, 130, 132
connection network, 23
Conservatives, vii, 5, 73, 89, 112, 113, 114, 115, 120, 121, 122, 129, 136–9, 144
constitution, 58, 96
consumerism, 16, 73, 117, 121
Copernicus, 94
corporatism, 3
corruption, 10, 16, 18–9, 20–2, 23–4,

## About the Author

A political scientist, Benedict Stavis has specialized in Chinese studies since 1963. He has taught and done academic research at several universities, including Cornell, Michigan State, and Harvard. He is currently at the Center for Asian and Pacific Studies at the University of Iowa. He has previously written books and numerous articles on various aspects of China's development. This book draws on his insights while teaching at China's Fudan University during the fall semester of 1986.